THE RIVER TEES

THE RIVER TEES

A North Country River

R. WOODHOUSE

Photographs by Dave Morrell

TERENCE DALTON LIMITED
LAVENHAM   .   SUFFOLK
1991

Published by

TERENCE DALTON LIMITED

ISBN 0 86138 091 6

Text photoset in 10/11pt Baskerville

Printed in Great Britain at
The Lavenham Press Limited, Lavenham, Suffolk

Contents

Index of Illustrations

Index of Maps

Dedicated to all those who share my
interest in, and affection for,
the many aspects of this fascinating river

Acknowledgements

MANY people have contributed a range of advice, information and practical assistance to the production of this book. Dave Morrell has provided all the photographs that are featured in the book, along with the colour slide that appears on the front cover, Alan Medd drew the maps that appear at the beginning of each chapter and Valerie Symonds has typed the text. I am deeply indebted to each of these friends for their prompt and efficient co-operation in supplying material of the highest quality, which made my work of co-ordinating the whole project so much simpler.

During the course of researching material, countless individuals have rendered considerable assistance in the form of written material and illustrative and photographic items, as well as practical advice and constructive suggestions. Numbered among these are past and present wardens of the nature reserves in Upper Teesdale, namely Paul Burnham, Terry Wells and Ian Findlay, and people with specific knowledge about locations and projects on the upper section of the Tees, including Tom Buffey, Dennis Coggins and Keith Watson. Other people who have provided valuable assistance on settlements along the river include Mrs L. D. Headlam-Morley (Whorlton), Mr W. Trudgill (Piercebridge), Mrs N. Evans (Worsall), Mr and Mrs T. Kidd (Worsall), Mr I. Graham (Thornaby).

Staff at Stockton, Middlesbrough and Darlington reference libraries have spent a considerable amount of time finding material and answering specific questions on many aspects of the river. Much background information on the lower reaches of the river was provided by Geoff Wicking and members of the staff of the Tees and Hartlepool Port Authority.

To these and many other unnamed groups and individuals, I remain extremely grateful.

R. Woodhouse
March, 1990

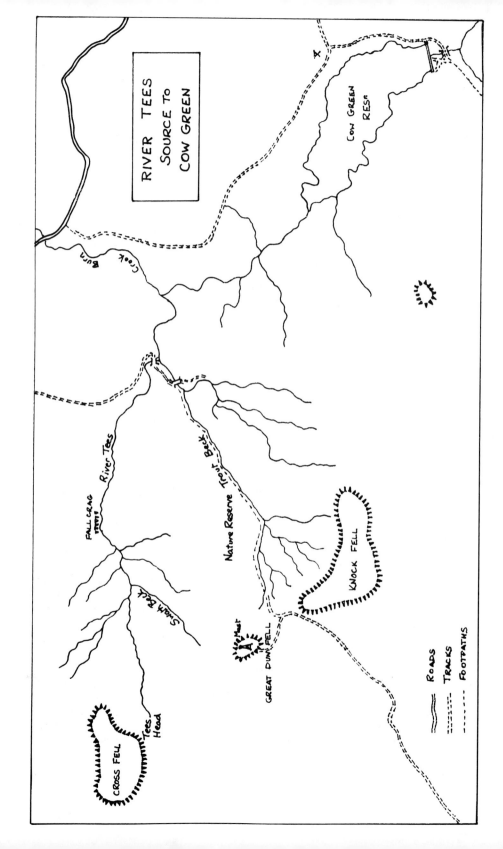

RIVER TEES
SOURCE TO
COW GREEN

Crook Burn

Cow GREEN RESr

River Tees

FALL CRAG

Nature Reserve

Trout Beck

KNOCK FELL

Sleath Beck

Tees Head

CROSS FELL

GREAT DUN FELL

Mast

ROADS
TRACKS
FOOTPATHS

CHAPTER ONE

From the Source to Cow Green Reservoir

T HE NORTH Pennine Dales contain some of this country's most spectacular scenery, and it is here on the eastern slopes of Cross Fell that the Tees begins its ninety-eight mile journey to the North Sea. Cross Fell is England's second highest mountain, with a height of 893 metres (2,930 feet) above sea level, and dominates the Pennine Range. It is said to have earned the title "Fiend's Fell" some 600 years ago when monks from Hexham erected a cross to exorcise local fiends. In 1747 a local botanist and surveyor, George Smith, provided the first detailed account of the ascent of an English mountain—Cross Fell.

The river's birthplace at Tees head is marked by a boundary stone with the letters "B/T" on the front and "F" on the reverse side, which indicate the extent of the Manors of Blencarn and Thanet, as well as Mr Fleming's land holdings. This location is remote, amidst a landscape that is barren and bleak but with a certain compelling appeal. The *Gentleman's Magazine* of 1847 summarized annual climatic conditions on Cross Fell as "ten months buried in snow and eleven in cloud" and though this is an obvious exaggeration, the air is usually damp and cool, with waterlogged conditions underfoot and a covering of snow for three months or more each winter. Frost is recorded at least once during every month of the year and the terrain is recognised by Swedish scientists as tundra conditions.

An unusual phenomenon is the Helm Wind, probably the most powerful and the coldest blast to be found anywhere in Britain. From a gathering point in the eastern section of this wild moorland, the savage wind sweeps across high ground to Cross Fell, where it blows at right angles to the scarp before plunging downwards in an icy blast. Wooden farm buildings on the western slopes of Cross Fell have often collapsed before the gale and although it has been credited with any number of unlikely feats, so far it defies detailed scientific explanation. In meteorological language, it is described as a Katabatic wind, meaning one that drops. Often accompanied by some form of cloud cap (as with the "table cloth" on the Table Mountain of South Africa), Cross Fell wears a "helmet" which gives rise to the name—Helm Wind.

The first scientific investigation was carried out in 1885, but produced no conclusive results. During 1937, Mr Gordon Manley of Durham University made regular observations from a location near the summit of Cross Fell, but during that period the Helm Wind failed to make a characteristic appearance.

Sheep were introduced to the northern hills by Norsemen some thousand years ago, but grazing in these parts is poor and each animal needs one hectare of land. Losses are severe during a harsh winter, but over the years sheep have been largely responsible for the disappearance of trees and shrubs.

1

Further changes to the landscape are a result of lead mining operations. Prospecting opencuts (commonly referred to as "hushes"), mine tips and drainage leats are found throughout this area, but even though these features and the mine buildings themselves are becoming less obvious, they still represent a hazard to unwary or inexperienced walkers.

The river itself spills through a series of rocky pools close to the source to cut a channel down a "V-shaped" valley, where it soon becomes a fair-sized beck that can no longer easily be crossed. As it twists and turns, banks have been eroded to form deep pools of peaty water with areas of shingle on the inside of the curves. In places there are miniature waterfalls, and then in contrast the high underwashed bank is capped by peat several metres thick, which rests on a layer of boulder clay and deeper beds of sandstone and shale. Lower levels show evidence of the limbs and trunks of trees to prove that the area was once woodland. Along other stretches the water has eaten into the joints of limestone outcrops to leave smoothly worn blocks full of pot holes separated by regular grooves. Some of the limestone is black, with its polished surface eroded into small pits and hollows rich in fossils.

A large area of land south of the Tees is now enclosed in the Moor House Nature Reserve. Nearly 4,000 hectares (10,000 acres) of moorland make up the largest such reserve in England, is situated south of Cross Fell. Purchased from the Appleby Castle Estate in 1952, the land had been used for common grazing for centuries. However, different mining activities have scarred the landscape, and more recently it served as a grouse moor.

The field station and warden's house, the latter being the highest occupied house in England, are sited within the reserve, which is some eleven kilometres south of the village of Garrigill. Included are laboratory and hostel facilities for visiting scientists. At 550 metres OD they provided an ideal base for moorland research and were used as the main United Kingdom site for measurements of terrestrial productivity in moorland systems for the International Biological Programme carried out between 1967 and 1972. Conditions on the reserve resemble those at sea-level in Iceland and a range of animal, plant and bird life thrives among the peat bogs, and shingle beds. The river's banks and small islands provide a habitat for golden plover, common sandpiper, dipper, oyster catcher and black-headed gull, while the moorland and higher rocky outcrops support curlew, kestrel, skylark, dunlin, wheatear and three pairs of whinchat. Cloudberry grows in profusion on the acid land that covers much of the reserve, while crowberry, blanket bog and heather cover the remaining areas.

Common lizard and frog thrive on the sectors of lush sphagnum moss, and plants such as lady's mantle, mountain pansy, milkwort and (after fire) the rose bay willow herb are to be found on this remote landscape. The reserve was

Opposite: The author at the boundary stone on the eastern slopes of Cross Fell which marks the source of the River Tees. It is shown on OS maps as Teeshead.

Great Dun Fell (left), Little Dun Fell (middle) and Cross Fell (right) viewed from Cow Green Reservoir. The source of the Tees lies in the hollow between Cross Fell and Little Dun Fell.

formed to facilitate research into upland moorland management and plots of land have been fenced off to study natural growth when sheep are excluded.

Trout Beck runs through the reserve to join the Tees from a south-westerly direction, and during severe weather in the winter of 1979–80 living conditions at the warden's accommodation became almost intolerable. Ice-floes and torrents of water ran off slopes as the area began to resemble an Alaskan landscape, and a bridge built of railway sleepers, which provided the only link with the outside world, had to be removed before it was carried away by the weight of ice and water.

The warden and his family were "snowed in" from 21st December 1979 to 21st April 1980 and soon afterwards moved to more hospitable surroundings in the Eden Valley, but even this forbidding environment supports alpine scurvy grass and alpine penny cress on the acid-tolerant soil of old mine workings, along with the mountain field pansy and the rare moonwort.

Names such as Rough Dike and Hard Hill indicate the nature of the terrain and abandoned mining heaps in this area are rich in fluorspar. Crook Burn joins the Tees close to Metalband Hill and here the river runs swiftly over a rocky bed that was formed by the Teesdale Glacier.

Until 1967 the Tees formed a swampy basin crossed by a deep winding pool known as the Weel which spread to the rim of the rocky outcrop at Cauldron Snout, but during the nineteen-sixties increased demands for water by industries on Teesside meant that a site had to be found for another reservoir. Reservoirs had already been constructed on two of the Tees' tributaries, the rivers Lune (Selset and Grassholme) and Balder (Balderhead, Blackton and Hury) so the waters of the Tees itself now had to be harnessed. A site at Dine Holm quarry above High Force was proposed, but this aroused great opposition and an alternative location was suggested in the Cow Green area. Again there was tremendous opposition from conservationists and scientists who objected to the loss of several species of rare alpine plant. A Teesdale Defence Fund was set up to fight the case, a Parliamentary enquiry was held and only after lengthy proceedings in both Houses of Parliament, with certain safeguards agreed, did the Cow Green Reservoir Scheme gain the Royal Assent on 22nd March, 1967.

ICI Ltd established a trust fund of £100,000 to allow investigation into aspects of scientific interest above High Force over a ten year period and the company also financed the appointment of an officer, Mr Tom Buffey, to safeguard the interests of local landowners, conservationists and the general public during construction work. Mr Buffey recalls a happy atmosphere on the construction site, which provided work for many local menfolk who were transported from the former railway station at Middleton-in-Teesdale each day. Brims and Company built the access road that ran below the planned top water level of the reservoir, while Mitchell Construction Company were the main contractors for the site. This remote landscape came alive in the late nineteen-sixties with all the sights and sounds of a major construction site, but at the end of November each year building work stopped and machinery and workforce moved out until weather conditions improved during the following spring. Design of the dam incorporated a concrete section made up of 22 blocks of 13.72 metres (45 feet) width and an earth embankment, along with a valve house at the toe of the dam which contains controls for regulating the discharge of water into the river. Over 222.7 hectares (550 acres) of land in this area contained arctic alpine vegetation, and with completion of the reservoir 41 of these acres were flooded. When full, the total surface water covers 311.8 hectares (770 acres) and holds over 40,000 million litres of water, which is supplied to Teesside throughout the year for industrial and domestic purposes thus using the river as an open pipe line.

At its deepest point, the water is 22.9 metres (75 feet deep), but it freezes over in winter, and extensive snowfall on nearby hills usually allows the Teesdale warden to carry out his duties on skis. The Upper Teesdale National Nature Reserve, for which he is responsible, covers 3,497 hectares (18,743 acres) of mainly sheepwalk and grouse moor. It was established by the Nature Conservancy, following agreements with the owners and their tenants—the Earl of Strathmore on the south side and Lord Barnard on the north side—in 1963 and 1969 respectively. In 1970, the Reserve was extended to include the eastern margin of Cow Green Reservoir from the Northumbrian Regional Water Authority, and it now attracts between 55,000 and 70,000 visitors annually with the greatest pressure during the months of May, June and July. A range of interesting flowering plants, ferns, mosses, liverworts and lichens have flourished in Upper Teesdale for at least twelve thousand years. The best known of these is the spring gentian, but the metamorphic limestone, which is unique to Teesdale, also provides an ideal habitat for the Teesdale violet and Teesdale sandwort. Metamorphic limestone when subjected to heat and pressure becomes marble. During this process the crystalline structure changes but the chemical composition remains the same.

Wild thyme, rock rose, harebell, bird's-foot trefoil and mountain pansy are common and there are rare species, such as autumn fellwort, hoary whitlow grass and hair sedge. Yellow sedge and carnation sedge thrive in the lime-rich environment, as does the rare false sedge, along with many rare or uncommon flowering plants, such as the bird's-eye primrose, Scottish asphodel and the insect-eating butterwort. The sticky leaves of the latter capture the prey, after which the plant produces digestive enzymes. Six thousand pairs of black-headed gull have settled at Cow Green, but typical upland birds nesting here include red grouse, golden plover, redshank, lapwing, curlew, wheatear, skylark and meadow pipit.

The climatological station at the Upper Teesdale National Nature Reserve is the highest in Great Britain. It contains nineteen different items of equipment, including a wind device, sun-dial, Stephenson screen, soil thermometer, rainfall gauge and acid rain gauge, and was installed in 1968 to facilitate scientific research by the Nature Conservancy Council and university students.

Research has shown that the reservoir has caused no change in temperature, but high winds have produced waves which in turn have eroded the shore-line of the reservoir. A period of dry weather during the summer of 1984 caused the reservoir level to drop, and this uncovered a previously unknown prehistoric settlement. Before the water rose and re-covered the site, excavations led by Mr Dennis Coggins from Bowes Museum investigated what is thought to be a farmstead dating from the Bronze Age Period.

Cow Green Reservoir has ample parking space for visitors and is within easy reach of the B6377 road from Middleton-in-Teesdale to Alston (Langdon Beck turn off). Visitors to the Nature Reserve must keep to the designated footpaths; from here, at a height of over 500 metres (1,805 feet) above sea level, there are fine views of Cross Fell, Mickle Fell and Great Dun Fell with its distinctive radio and radar equipment.

Information for walkers

A bridle way from the village of Blencarn leads up the south western slopes of Cross Fell to a point very close to the source of the Tees before linking up with the Pennine Way as it runs northwards from Cross Fell towards Alston. This route offers superb views over the surrounding countryside on a clear day.

There are no public rights of way along the banks of the Tees below its source, and this sector of land south of the river is enclosed within the Moor House National Nature Reserve.

In 1973 Durham County Council produced a proposal for a Teesdale Way Long Distance Footpath, covering 72 miles from Harwood Common on the B6277 Barnard Castle–Alston road to Yarm (with possible extensions at either end). Work on the Teesdale Way is now well advanced. The section to Middleton-in-Teesdale opened in 1991, and work on the sections between Barnard Castle and Darlington and downstream are to be completed during 1992 and 1993.

The upper section of Cauldron Snout. Its series of rocky steps form England's largest cascade.

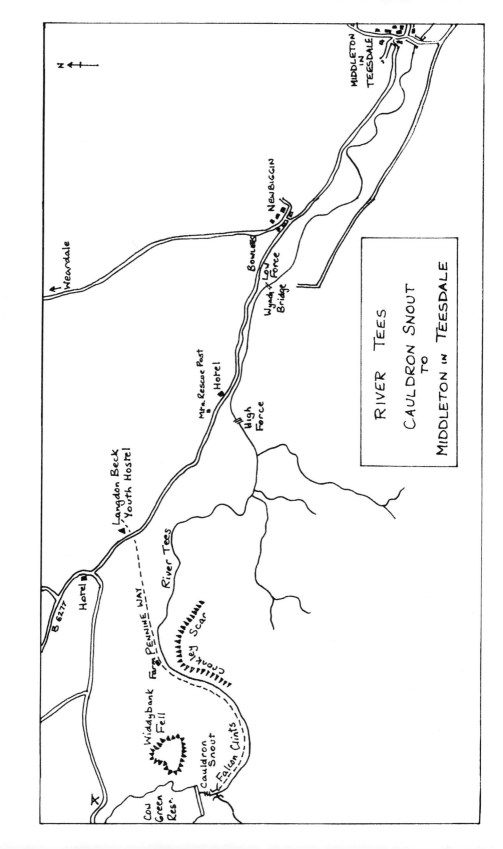

CHAPTER TWO

Cauldron Snout to Middleton-in-Teesdale

A SHORT distance below Cow Green Reservoir, the river crosses a band of igneous rock known as the Whin Sill to create England's longest and largest cataract—Cauldron Snout. Rocks lining the channel compare in form with the organ pipes of the Giant's Causeway and the foaming waters drop approximately eighty feet as they cascade through a series of eight falls that spread along a length of 366 metres (1,200 feet). The well-worn footpath along the river's eastern side provides a dramatic encounter with the torrent as it speeds through the rapids, and serves as a reminder of the legend of the Singing Lady of Cauldron Snout. Events surrounding this tale date back to the last century, when lead and barytes were mined nearby and the labour force lived for days on end in "mine shops" close to the workings. A young country girl who was employed to carry out domestic chores in a building not far from Cauldron Snout fell in love with one of the miners, but the love affair came to a sudden end when the miner returned home to his family. Shortly afterwards the girl is said to have made her way to the edge of the falls and thrown herself into the torrent. Local folklore indicates that can still be seen at night beside the rocky outcrop, singing her sad love song.

Below Cauldron Snout, the Tees is joined from the west by Maize Beck at a point where the counties of Durham, Yorkshire and Cumberland formerly met. The Pennine Way joins the Tees here and the river enters one of its most impressive sections, with the 30.5 metre (100 foot) cliffs of Falcon Clints and Cronkley Scar forcing the surging river into a bouldery channel. Small birches and juniper bushes represent the first trees below the source on Cross Fell and the valley widens a little as the river approaches Widdybank Farm. Most of the scattered stone buildings on neighbouring slopes are whitewashed, and Widdybank's walls stand out clearly against the dark shades of the fell-side. Its construction and layout is typical of many of the farmsteads in Upper Teesdale with hay barn, cow byre and farmhouse under one roof, but since becoming part of one of the largest farms in Teesdale the farmhouse has not been regularly inhabited. Drainage schemes and the application of lime and fertilizer have improved both pasture and hayfields in the Widdybank area. A flock of Swaledale sheep are reared on the open moorland and during the summer months a herd of approximately seventy cross Galloway and Aberdeen Angus beef cattle graze in the fields.

Many farms in Upper Teesdale began as smallholdings cultivated by local lead miners in their spare time. Landowners allowed miners to claim small enclosures on the edge of moorland, which became known as "intakes"; farms with this name are quite common. There is now no trace of a former pencil mill that stood close by the south side of the river. It produced slate pencils, which were known locally as "widdies".

Langdon Beck Youth Hostel is a convenient starting point for exploration of Teesdale's upper reaches. The building was reconstructed after a serious fire in 1958. Nearby Langdon Common is said to be one of the windiest locations in the country, and this has led to plans for a "wind farm" where the power of the gales can be harnessed to produce electricity for the National Grid.

Downstream from Cronkley Bridge, the river bends through banks lined with a miniature forest of juniper bushes. This sturdy evergreen shrub with thickly spreading branches proved useful to local folk in earlier days. Chips of juniper wood were used to fumigate houses in times of plague or sickness and the berries can be used for flavouring gin. On the northern bank stone is blasted from sheer rock faces to provide material for road-making. Quarry buildings mar the river landscape along this stretch, but the operation provides much-needed employment for local people.

High Force

The river gathers speed as it approaches Teesdale's best known attraction—High Force. A belt of deciduous woodland lines the northern bank as the waters race through a rocky channel to the edge of England's largest waterfall. This dramatic feature is formed by a thick layer of fine-grained igneous rock called dolerite—better known locally as whinstone—which crosses the river at this point, causing the Tees to fall almost eighty feet into a plunge pool at the head of the gorge. Since the completion of Cow Green Reservoir in 1971, the river's flow has been reduced and it is only in times of extreme flooding that the whole face is covered. For most of the time only the southern fall operates and in summer thousands of tourists visit this superb natural attraction, most of them making the short walk from the roadside close to the High Force Hotel. During harsh winters, High Force has frozen into a glistening curtain, but it is during the summer months that most sightseers crowd the rocky outcrops around the fall. Great care should be taken at this beauty spot, for in recent years several people have fallen to their deaths in the High Force area.

Migratory salmon reached the pool at the foot of High Force in earlier years and from here the river flows in a long straight channel that cuts into the Whin Sill. About two miles downstream from High Force the river tumbles over another of Teesdale's most scenic attractions—Low Force, which has also been known as Little Force and Salmon Leap. Situated some 250 yards from the road and adjacent to the Pennine Way, this series of low falls attracts crowds of sightseers during the summer months. The rocky pools are a favourite location with visitors, but the current is strong along this stretch as the waters gather before surging through a narrow gorge crossed by the Winch Bridge. This

Opposite page: England's largest waterfall, High Force viewed from the southern bank.

Salmon Leap close to the Winch Bridge at Low Force. The Tees was one of the country's finest salmon rivers, and as pollution levels are reduced salmon should soon return to its upper reaches.

slender suspension bridge, first opened in 1830, replaced a much older structure dating from 1704, said to be the first of its kind in England. This early bridge was used by local lead miners on their way to Holwick, and, having a hand rail on one side only, it was described by Hutchinson, a Durham historian, as "planked in such a manner that the traveller experiences all the tremulous motion of the chains and sees himself suspended over a roaring gulf on an agitated restless gangway to which few strangers dare trust themselves". In 1803 the main chain broke when a group of miners were crossing and one man was drowned.

Evidence of occupation dating back some six thousand years has been uncovered in nearby fields and mesolithic flints are still found in this area. In 1976 Durham County Council opened a visitor centre in a reclaimed limestone quarry close to the Bowlees Beck. Situated about half a mile from the Tees, it is within easy walking distance of Gibson's Cave—an amazing recess in the hard limestone outcrop. In the past vast volumes of water pouring over the limestone outcroppings has produced a bewildering variety of shapes.

A number of footpaths lead from Winch Bridge, and apart from the copses of hazel, poplar and birch that are found on the south bank, there are several

Winch Bridge spans a rocky gorge close to the village of Newbiggin in Teesdale.

species of flowers, including bird's-eye primrose, mountain pansy, rock rose, globe flower and autumn gentian, while tufts of the large yellow shrub cinque foil grow among the stones at the water's edge.

The tiny hamlet of Holwick was a busy local centre at the height of the mining era, but it enjoys quieter times today. Farmers, quarrymen and gamekeepers reared their families here and formed a community which centred on the school, inn and chapel. There was also talk in these parts of ghosts and bogles, but this may well have been a ploy by parents to deter children from venturing near the riverside or from staying out after darkness fell. Park End Quarry ceased operation long ago, but when in use rock was blasted from the face to be used as paving blocks or road-making materials. The stone and workforce were transported to and from nearby Middleton-in-Teesdale, but in recent years these old industries have closed and families have moved away, leaving their former homes to be converted into holiday retreats.

These early days of industry and activity in Teesdale are recalled in graphic detail through the writings of Richard Watson. Born at Middleton-in-Teesdale on 16 May, 1833, he had a brief period at school before going to work in the lead mines at the age of ten. His father died a few years later and Richard spent the rest of his life as a lead miner supporting his mother and six sisters.

The London Lead Mining Company played a major role in the social structure of the district. Miners in the company's employment were expected to attend a place of worship on Sundays and to ensure that their children were at services; they could lose their jobs for drunkenness, brawling or other offences, but in return for following the company's regulations they received benefits that were otherwise unknown at the time. A fund was set up to give financial support to miners who were maimed in accidents or crippled by ill-health, for work in the lead mining industry was physically demanding, dangerous and unhealthy. Underground operations brought the obvious dangers of roof collapse, flooding or explosion, along with the effects of lead poisoning. In spite of these hazardous conditions, wage levels were low and there were long periods of unemployment.

Richard Watson's writings explain aspects of mining life and indicate contemporary attitudes. "My Journey to Work" is a description of the seven-mile walk from Holwick to Little Eggleshope Mine on a Monday morning after the weekend has been spent at home. Along the way he picks out the natural beauty of the hills and fells as well as describing mining activity at Colberry and Wiregill Mines. "The Miner's Sabbath Morning" gives details of family life at the weekend while touches of humour centre on the mishaps that befall unpopular local characters. Other elements that emerge from Watson's writings are humility and acceptance of the class system in society as well as a staunch patriotism. Above all, he exhibits a great affection for the natural beauty and traditions of Teesdale with its changing seasons and different moods.

The river races over a wide stony channel as it approaches Middleton-in-Teesdale, which became the centre for mining operations and business activity in the upper sector of Teesdale during the nineteenth century.

Information for walkers

There is ample car parking space at Cow Green Reservoir and a well-marked footpath leads walkers along the northern bank around the barrage towards Cauldron Snout.

The vertical sections of rock at Cauldron Snout are fairly difficult to negotiate (especially in wet weather), but below the cascade the ground becomes more level and from the confluence of the Tees with the Maize Beck the Pennine Way runs along the banks of the Tees for several miles.

Outcrops of fallen rocks make walking difficult in places, but the boots of countless hikers are gradually wearing away the awkward angles of these boulders. In other places duckboards have been provided to enable walkers to cross waterlogged sections.

The Pennine Way is clearly marked as it passes Widdybank Farm, crosses Langdon Beck and then crosses the Tees at Cronkley Bridge. It runs over High Crag and follows the southern bank along the section past High Force and Low Force into Middleton-in-Teesdale.

Northern bank of the Tees below Cauldron Snout looking towards Falcon Clints. The Pennine Way runs along the stretch of river between Cauldron Snout and Middleton in Teesdale.

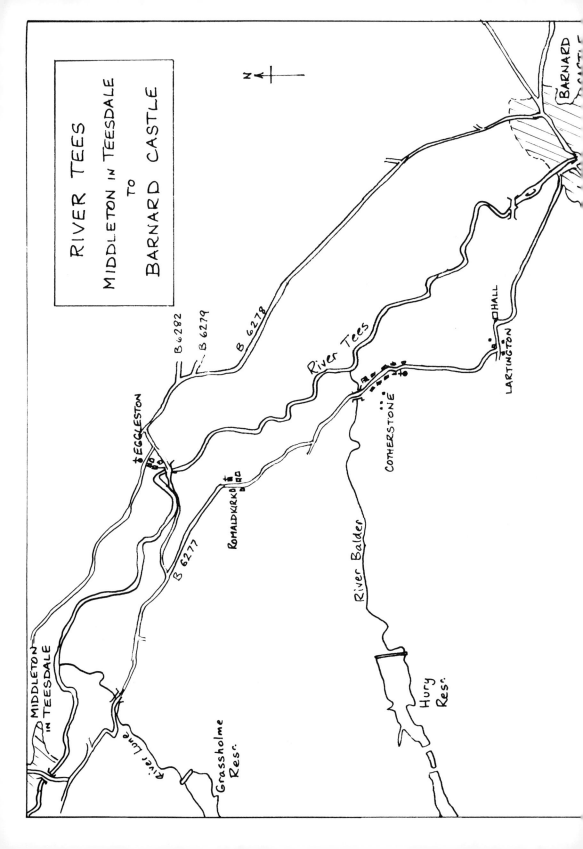

RIVER TEES
MIDDLETON IN TEESDALE
TO
BARNARD CASTLE

N

BARNARD CASTLE

B 6282
B 6279
B 6278

River Tees

HALL

LARTINGTON

EGGLESTON

COTHERSTONE

ROMALDKIRK

B 6277

River Balder

MIDDLETON IN TEESDALE

River Lune

Grassholme Resr.

Hury Resr.

CHAPTER THREE

Middleton-in-Teesdale to Barnard Castle

MIDDLETON-IN-TEESDALE is a spreading market town on a terrace of land above the river's highest flood levels. Its layout reflects the tone of the area, with solid stone buildings offering shelter from harsh winter weather and refreshment for tourists and hikers during the summer months. Land rises steeply behind the town, which was in earlier days a self-contained centre with a variety of shops and services as well as fairs and shows and a market on Saturdays and Tuesdays.

The parish church, dedicated to St Mary the Virgin, dates from 1876, but there have been church buildings on this same site for over eight hundred years. Richard Watson, Teesdale's poet, is buried within the churchyard, which also contains the only detached bellhouse in the Diocese of Durham. This curious structure dates from 1557 and was bequeathed by the Reverend William Bell. The three original bells were rung by one man, who pulled on the ropes with both hands and a foot.

County Bridge was completed in 1853 using funds raised by public subscription. It replaced an earlier bridge dating from 1811 which had collapsed before being completed. A local butcher, Richard Attee, regularly predicted an early end to the bridge's life; one day he was pointing out its defects from below when the structure gave way, fatally injuring both Mr Attee and his wife. The present bridge has an unusual design feature with circular holes at each side—included in order to reduce the weight of the arches. Severe frosts during the early months of 1982 seriously weakened much of the stonework and extensive repairs were carried out during 1983–84. At this time traffic used a Bailey bridge constructed alongside the single-arched stone bridge.

Everyday life in Middleton was revolutionized by the arrival of the London Lead Mining Company in 1815. A number of buildings survive from prosperous mining days and these include the distinctive clock tower housed in Masterman Place and dated 1824 and the company's head office, which is now privately owned. A drinking fountain, which stands close to the centre of the township, was erected in 1875 using proceeds from a retirement collection for Robert Walton Bainbridge, the company superintendent. A total of £262 15s 5d was donated and after presents had been purchased the surplus cash was used to pay for the fountain. The company helped to set up a village band, a horticultural society and annual show, along with a range of educational activities revolving around Sunday schools and church-going.

Hamlets such as Newbiggin and Eggleston were enlarged as the company developed its mining activities during the nineteenth century, and larch and fir trees were planted on moorland areas so that they could be felled for use as

props in the mines. New roads were built by the mining company and "trods" linked the more remote workings as life was revolutionized in this quiet corner of Northern England. There had been a long history of mineral workings in the northern dales before the 1800s and it is likely that the Romans quarried into the hills of Upper Teesdale. Documentary references to silver and lead mining in these parts date back to the fifteenth century and early prospectors may well have used the method known as "hushing" to expose a workable vein. The most prominent example of this method is at Redgroves near Newbiggin. It can be clearly seen from the road that runs through the village on the way to High Force—as a gap on the northern ridge of the valley side. Hushing involved blocking a stream high on the fellside and then releasing the torrent of water in order to sweep away surface soil and loose stones, leaving the underlying strata exposed. Other prospectors scoured the hillsides in search of lead-tolerant plants.

As workings became scattered across the countryside "mine shops" or lodging houses were set up for the workforce. A mine shop and other features of a lead mine have been carefully restored at Killhope in Weardale and represent the most complete surviving lead mining site in Britain. The workings are situated thirteen miles from Stanhope and are open daily from mid-March to the end of October. This system began in 1818; the rough dwellings offered little comfort to miners, who left home on a Monday morning and stayed there until the following Saturday morning, along with thirty or forty fellow workers. Bunks lined with straw were crammed into these solid stone buildings and miners cooked on a communal fire but using their own utensils. A working week spanned forty hours, made up of eight-hour shifts; candles provided light for miners, who drilled holes in the ore and then packed in explosives to blast out mineral deposits. The ore was loaded on to horse-drawn bogies which conveyed it along rails to the mine entrance, where it was tipped into stone bunkers. From there it was moved to the picking floors for men and boys to sort out larger lumps. The remaining bits were moved to the crushing mill, which was driven by a water-wheel. Lighter materials were washed away and the ore was stored in readiness for transportation to the smelt mill. A large amount of water was needed for these operations; it was gathered in a reservoir above the workings and then channelled to each location.

Miners were paid on a piece-work basis at the end of a three months' contract and during this period they could borrow from the Company on "lend days". At times a miner borrowed more than he had earned during the preceding quarter and this added to the other hardships that resulted from hazardous working conditions. Some underground workers negotiated their wages from a bargain system and received an average of fifty shillings per month. The harsh and unhealthy conditions in workings and mine shops led to outbreaks of disease and violence.

Opposite page: A family by the drinking fountain at Middleton in Teesdale. Public donations paid for the fountain, which is a memorial to an official of the London Lead Mining Company.

The township of Middleton-in-Teesdale became largely self-sufficient during the nineteenth century, but on 12th May, 1868, the Tees Valley Railway was extended from the Tees Valley Junction west of Barnard Castle to the edge of the community. The railway buildings of Middleton frequently won awards in the best-kept station competition, but following closure of the line to passengers in November, 1964, and to goods in April, 1965, the premises were occupied by a coal merchant and lost their original attractiveness.

Lead mining declined in Upper Teesdale towards the end of the nineteenth century and in 1905 the London Lead Mining Company went bankrupt in the face of cheap imported ores. As unemployment spread, many families left the area in search of work and the population fell from about 2,000 to around 1,300. Some mining enterprises were re-started as barytes was found to have a value, but in recent years Swiss Aluminium Mining UK has been the only company to be actively engaged in excavating minerals in the area.

Eggleston

Eggleston village stands on high ground along the Tees' northern bank, a short distance downstream from Middleton. Everyday life was revolutionized during mining days at nearby Blackton, but quieter times have returned to this attractive collection of houses. Eggleston Hall was built for William Hutchinson in 1820 with design work carried out by Ignatius Bonomi. More recently it has become the Gray family's ancestral home and since the early nineteen-seventies it has been the setting for a range of cookery courses run by Mrs Rosemarie Gray. This square stone-built mansion has an impressive Greek colonnade of five fluted columns and the beautiful gardens are regularly opened to the public.

A large stone, known as the Bacon or Bawcock Stone, marks the place where farm produce was deposited and then paid for during an outbreak of the plague. The victims left their money in the depression in the stone, which was filled with vinegar; the rough and ready method of disinfection almost certainly worked.

Percymyre Rock is featured in folklore as the spot where a member of the Fitzhugh family, Lords of Cotherstone, tumbled over the edge as his horse chased a deer close to the edge of this sheer outcrop.

Eggleston Bridge is said to be five hundred years old, but long-term deterioration was made worse by severe frosts in the early nineteen-eighties and extensive repair work was needed. The structure was closed to traffic throughout 1982 as a concrete saddle was inserted and external stonework replaced; the overall appearance of this narrow, two-arched structure fortunately remains unaltered.

During the early nineteen-eighties Northumbrian Water Authority completed a tunnel network which enabled water to be transferred from Kielder Water to the River Tees via the Wear Valley. The Eggleston outlet for this system is situated a short distance downstream from the bridge and blends well into the river bank.

View of the Tees between Eggleston and Cotherstone.

Romaldkirk

The river enters one of its most attractive stretches below Eggleston with small boulders forming an uneven channel as it flows past Romaldkirk. An assortment of stone cottages cluster around the green to form a compact little village dominated by a large church which has been called the Cathedral of the Dales. Dedicated to an unknown saint—Romald—who may have been a Northumbrian prince, it probably stands on the site of a Saxon church. Scottish raiders destroyed early buildings, but parts of the present church date from the twelfth and thirteenth centuries while the west tower with its vaulted roof is of fifteenth-century origin. Parish registers date back to 1578 and include details of a terrible outbreak of the plague which struck Northern England in 1644. A miller is blamed for bringing the infection to Romaldkirk on his return from Newcastle-upon-Tyne, and as the death rate soared villagers were buried in communal graves close to the river. Few people survived the outbreak. One who did survive was Grace Scott, who left her home in the village and built a turf hut about a mile away. She is said to have remained there until the plague had passed.

The public footpath from Romaldkirk to Cotherstone on the southern bank passes through a field known as Woden Croft. Some experts link this area with Norse settlers and their gods, but the nearby farmhouse, Woden Croft Lodge, has more recent connections. It was a boarding school of the type described by Dickens in *Nicholas Nickleby*, and numbered among its famous old boys is Richard Cobden, who spent five years of his school life here. He went on to become a leading figure in the campaign to abolish the Corn Laws, and the successful outcome in 1846 not only brought cheaper bread, but also marked a stage in the Free Trade Movement. The removal of duties and tariffs on various goods had begun in the late seventeen-hundreds by Pitt's government and both Huskisson and Peel had removed other goods prior to 1846. It was virtually completed by Gladstone in the late nineteenth century.

Cotherstone

The River Balder joins the Tees at Cotherstone and an adjacent sector of level ground is known as the Hagg—which means a cleared place in the forest. Beyond this area of open land the ground rises steeply and the hilltop marks the site of Cotherstone Castle. Little is known about the building, but early fortifications probably date from shortly after the Norman Conquest. Stonework was added in 1200, when King John granted a licence for building work, but it is not known how long the Castle was occupied. Scottish raiding parties are blamed for destruction of the Castle buildings, but it seems certain that much of the stonework was re-used in other local premises. Cotherstone, like many other minor castle, was used as an unofficial quarry.

Cotherstone itself is a long straggling settlement with buildings grouped around two greens. A network of paths and passageways links different parts of the village, which is surrounded by good farmland. Down the years many local people have been closely associated with dairy farming, and a well known local product is Cotherstone cheese. The Friends' Meeting House was built in 1797 and for many years there was a strong Quaker following in Cotherstone, while Romaldkirk had a large number of Anglicans, Middleton-in-Teesdale was mainly Wesleyan and Lartington enjoyed considerable Roman Catholic support.

Bridge at Cotherstone close to the confluence of the Tees and Balder.

Lartington

Lartington lies about a mile downstream from Cotherstone and this small village is dominated by the Hall, which was first established in the reign of Charles I. For centuries it was the home of the Maire family, but in 1830 it was acquired by the Witham family. Thomas Witham extended the building and added a splendid ballroom and elaborate coach porch, but during this century the hall was largely neglected until Robin Rackham moved in during the early nineteen-eighties and began an extensive restoration programme. Squash courts were set up in the chapel and ballroom to provide income for the ongoing improvements. Water treatment works at Lartington were opened in 1901. Impounding reservoirs in Lunedale and Baldersdale supplied the water, which originally passed through slow sand filters over 2.7 hectares (6.7 acres). A second method involves the use of rapid gravity filters, and as demand for drinking water increased, improvement works were carried out in the mid-nineteen-sixties.

Further improvements were made between 1983 and1985 at a cost of £1¼ million to provide new clarification tanks and a new chemical house as well as better sludge-collecting facilities, roadways and pipework.

Startforth

Startforth is just across the river from Barnard Castle. The village church was largely rebuilt in the nineteenth century, but older features include a fifteenth-century font and the worn figure of a woman with long neck and tiny face. This may represent Helen de Hastings who gave land to nearby Egglestone Abbey. An early educational establishment—Mr Kirkbride's Academy—was based in Startforth, but following a visit by Charles Dickens in 1838 there was a storm of protest against these "Do-The-Boys Schools" and closure soon followed.

Barnard Castle

Until recent years the riverside at Barnard Castle was dominated by a number of large mill buildings and run-down housing, but demolition and clearance schemes have opened up the area close to the bridge. On the southern bank Ullathorne Mill overshadowed most of the surrounding area. It was established in 1760 and specialized in production of shoelaces and ropes, but following closure in 1932 the building became derelict and it was finally demolished in 1976. Barnard Castle bridge dates from 1569 (not 1596 as a plaque incorrectly states) and until 1771 it included a chapel where illicit weddings were carried out on payment of a fee of 2s 6d. A serious flood in that year caused widespread damage all along the Tees and the two-ribbed and pointed arches of the bridge needed substantial repairs. The mellow brown stonework also includes a massive central pier to withstand high water levels, but in recent years the structure has been seriously weakened by heavy traffic. For many years traffic has been restricted to single line and a bypass for the town is still under consideration.

The town's Castle dominates the skyline above the bridge and down the centuries its dramatic outline has attracted a series of writers and artists, including Scott, Turner and Cotman. Early building work probably began before 1100 on the orders of Guy de Baliol, but both Castle and township take their name from his nephew, Bernard, who consolidated the Castle in stone. It remained in the hands of the Baliols during the twelfth and thirteenth centuries before passing to Bishop Bek of Durham, the Neville family and Sir Harry Vane, whose descendants assumed the title of Lord Barnard. It was the Baliol family who instituted the Oxford college. Barnard Castle became one of the largest castles in Northern England, but in spite of its chequered ownership, the inhabitants enjoyed a largely peaceful existence. During 1569 the Castle played a part in religious troubles, known as the Rising of the North when Sir George Bowes held it for the Queen. In spite of a severe shortage of food and water, the garrison resisted for eleven days. The Rising of the North was part of the religious turmoil which took place in the region of Queen Elizabeth I. Catholic forces led by the Earls of Northumberland and Westmorland besieged the castle

Bridge and castle at Barnard Castle. Baliol Tower is clearly seen within the castle's perimeter walls.

as part of an abortive campaign in support of Mary Queen of Scots' claim to the English throne. By 1648 the Castle was said to be in a ruinous condition and many of the adjacent properties were constructed with stone taken from buildings within the Castle precincts. In 1952 ownership passed to the Ministry of Works and the Castle is currently administered by English Heritage. The area within the curtain walls is divided into four wards and most material remains date from the period 1250–1350.

A thriving township grew up around the Castle and it developed into a considerable market and industrial centre. During the seventeenth century the emphasis was on farming, tanning, glove and stocking-making, but a hundred years later the woollen industry brought work and wealth to Barnard Castle. Some fine Georgian houses survive from this era, but as trends changed so carpet-weaving flourished during the nineteenth century and the Teesbank area was packed with factories, mills, workshops and domestic housing. The last carpet factory closed in 1870, but Thorngate Mill, opened in 1827, continued to produce worsted until 1973. The town's best-known landmark is the octagonal market cross built in 1747 by Thomas Breaks, a native of the town. Down the years it has had many uses—during the early eighteen-hundreds it was used as a town hall, a small room upstairs served as a court room and part of the lower level was adapted as a jail. At one time dairy produce was sold from the ground-level verandah. There is a curious explanation for the two holes that appeared in the weather vane during 1804. As they left the nearby Turks Head Inn, a local gamekeeper and a volunteer soldier began arguing about who was the best marksman and the weather vane, at a distance of about one hundred yards, was chosen as a target. The dispute was unresolved, for both men succeeded in hitting the vane.

Charles Dickens stayed at the King's Head during February, 1838, whilst gathering material for his novel, *Nicholas Nickleby*, and a clock-making business across the road provided inspiration for another book—*Master Humphrey's Clock*. Just below the market cross is the late sixteenth-century Blagraves House. It has

Barnard Castle's Butter Cross dominates the centre of the township. Down the years it has served as market cross and law court.

a prominent three-storeyed gabled bay with leaded windows and on the wall are four little figures of men playing musical instruments. According to local folklore, Oliver Cromwell was entertained in the building on 24th October, 1648 and is said to have feasted on mulled wine and shortcake. There are many other features of interest among the alleys, passages and cobbled yards and in recent years several of the town's buildings have been restored by the Teesdale Preservation Trust.

In 1969 the Council for British Archaeology designated Barnard Castle as the second most important historic settlement in County Durham—after Durham City—and its crowning glory is the magnificent Bowes Museum. John Bowes of Streatlam Castle began work on the building of the museum in November, 1869, but both he and his French wife had died before this superb French-style chateau was completed in 1892. Set in parkland of twenty-one acres, it now houses some of Europe's finest art treasures, including paintings from France, Spain, Italy and the Netherlands. There are large study collections of ceramics and textiles as well as Continental furniture, tapestries, clocks and objets d'art in period settings. Recent additions include displays of English furniture, silver, costume, toys and local antiquities, but the museum's unique attraction is the silver swan automaton. Made in the eighteenth century by an English craftsman named Weekes, it swims over a sea of glass rods and bends its neck to gather up fish. Previous owners of this amazing piece of engineering include Napoleon III, who bought it as a toy for the Prince Imperial.

Close to Bowes Museum stands Barnard Castle School, built between 1883 and 1886 with pupils based in premises at Middleton One Row from September, 1883, until completion of the buildings. Over the years the school has maintained a fine record of academic and sporting achievements. From this high vantage point on the west side of the town there are superb views across the course of the River Tees.

Information for walkers

Durham County Council have carried out improvements to the course of the old railway line from Middleton-in-Teesdale to Mickleton and Romaldkirk. Access points are clearly sign-posted from the roadside and this represents the best route (as opposed to following the B6277 into Romaldkirk).

A footpath opposite Romaldkirk church leads away from the village and heads left towards the river bank at Low Garth. It continues along the high ground above the wooded bank, passing Woden Croft, crossing Wilden Beck and running alongside a fence to cross the River Balder close to Cotherstone.

There is a choice of foothpaths—along either bank—between Cotherstone and Barnard Castle. My own preference is for the route along the northern bank which is reached from a footbridge just above the confluence with the River Balder. It runs through rough pastureland, along the edge of fields and through wooded slopes into Barnard Castle, passing the remnants of the railway viaduct and an early spa.

Walkers will find Ordnance Survey sheet 92 useful at this point.

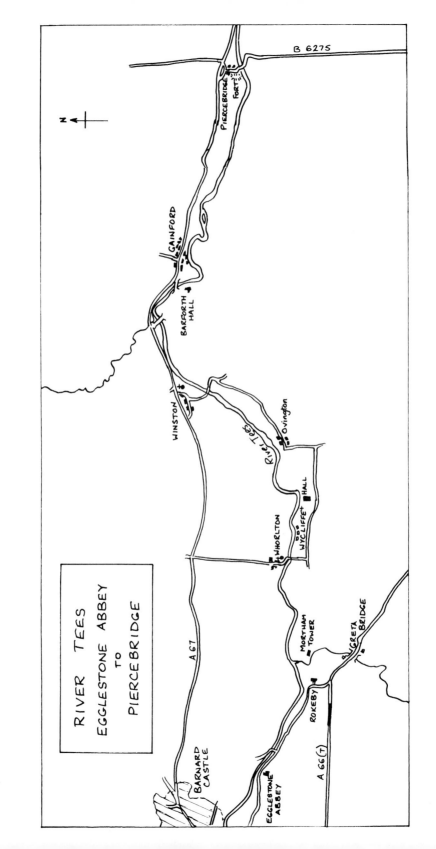

RIVER TEES
EGGLESTONE ABBEY
TO
PIERCEBRIDGE

CHAPTER FOUR

Egglestone Abbey to Piercebridge

BELOW Barnard Castle the river enters its most romantic section. Gently sloping grassland borders both banks, and little more than a mile downstream roads from both sides of the river converge near the ruins of the Premonstratensian Abbey of Egglestone. The Abbey stands on a terrace overlooking the Tees, cut off by the little beck of Thorsgill, which is crossed by a curious seventeenth-century packhorse bridge, and here a community of no more than fifteen white-robed monks lived out their life of service and solitude. Dedicated to St Mary and St John the Baptist, it was founded in 1195 by Ralph de Multon for monks from Easby Abbey near Richmond, North Yorkshire. The peace and tranquillity of this delightful setting was shattered twice during the fourteenth century, first at the hands of Scottish raiders in 1323 and again in 1346 as English troops plundered the Abbey before moving eastwards to defeat the Scots in battle at Neville's Cross near Durham. Henry VIII's commissioners dissolved the Abbey on 5th January, 1540, and many of the buildings were either dismantled or converted into dwellings before Major H. Morritt placed the ruins in the care of the Commissioners of Works in 1925. Materials were returned to the site and these included the splendidly carved tomb of Sir Ralph Bowes from nearby Mortham. It is possible to trace the ground plan of buildings in the north and west ranges but the remains in the east range are more extensive because this section was converted into a dwelling house. Sir Walter Scott was a regular visitor to Rokeby, which lies a short distance downstream from the Abbey, and soon after his first stay in 1809 he began work on a romantic poem, "Rokeby". Completed in 1812, it describes Egglestone Abbey in the following terms:

> The reverend pile lay wild and waste,
> Profaned, dishonour'd and defaced,
> Through storied lattices no more
> In soften'd light the sunbeams pour,
> Gilding the Gothic sculpture rich
> Of shrine and monument and niche.

Today the Abbey ruins are cared for by English Heritage with public access at all times. Looking down on the superb river scenery it is easy to visualize white-robed monks herding their cattle in nearby fields, before we take in the beauty of nearby Abbey Bridge.

The ruins of Egglestone Abbey dominate the river's southern skyline a short distance downriver from Barnard Castle.

Built in 1773 by J. B. S. Morritt, the bridge's single arch carries the roadway some 76 feet above the brown waters of the Tees. Ledges of "Teesdale marble" line both banks and in earlier times this grey limestone formation was quarried and worked by local craftsmen. Until about forty years ago travellers were charged a toll for using the bridge with amounts ranging from sixpence for cars to a halfpenny for pedestrians, one penny for bicycles and a fixed sum for each type of domestic animal. The toll collector and his family lived in two little buildings at the southern end of the bridge with a living room and kitchen on one side of the road and a bedroom on the other side. They had battlements and ornamental arrow loops to match the design of the bridge, but sadly both buildings have been demolished since the Second World War.

According to Leland, it is "two miles of pasture, corn and woode" from Egglestone to the delightful natural beauty of Greta Bridge. This spot is where the River Greta joins the Tees and down the years it has attracted a succession of writers and artists to record its charming features.

The Morritt family purchased nearby Rokeby Hall in 1769 and during the early eighteen-hundreds John Bacon Morritt forged a friendship with Walter Scott. Scott and his wife stayed at Rokeby Hall in June, 1809, and again in 1812 and it was during this latter visit that he completed the thirty-thousand-word poem known as "Rokeby" referred to above. Published on 1st January, 1813, the first edition sold quickly, and though generally considered to be inferior to his other works, it does describe in detail the splendours of this area of Teesdale. A short distance away from Rokeby Hall stands Mortham Tower, the most southerly of the Border peel towers. The present building dates from the fifteenth century and is said to be haunted by "Mortham Dobby", a fine lady with a piece of white silk trailing after her. There are several explanations of the apparition, the most popular one stating that the spectre is a Lady Rokeby who was shot by robbers as she walked in the woods and who now returns to haunt the building.

Whorlton

About a mile downstream from Rokeby, and on the northern bank, lies the peaceful village of Whorlton. Buildings stand on the north and south sides of a wide green with the small church occupying the south eastern corner. A chapel of ease that stood on the site was demolished in 1853 and replaced by the existing building with seating for 150 worshippers. A small bell tower— geometrical in shape and topped by an octagonal spirelet—houses a single bell, and memorial windows incorporated between 1865 and 1882 are dedicated to notable local people, including several members of the Headlam family. One of these left the area to become Bishop of Gloucester, and just before his term as Vicar (1854–76) the Reverend A. W. Headlam built Whorlton Hall. Standing adjacent to the church, it has 30 rooms, 17 bedrooms and five staircases and now provides accommodation for mentally handicapped adults. Other notable features around the green include the old school building bearing the date 1848, an ornate drinking fountain that was provided in 1887 on the occasion of Queen

31

The single-arched Abbey Bridge spans the gorge close to Egglestone Abbey. This stretch of the river is popular with canoeists.

Victoria's Golden Jubilee and the Independent Chapel (opened in 1840), which now serves as the village's community centre. A large red-brick building at the southern end of the village was used as the vicarage from 1890 until 1973, when it passed into private ownership. At this point the road narrows to restrict the flow of vehicles on the hill that drops steeply towards the bridge over the Tees. Begun in August 1830, the bridge spans 198 feet and retains the wrought iron chains and stone piers designed by John and Benjamin Green of Newcastle-upon-Tyne. An attractive toll house is sited at the northern end of the bridge, and although tolls are no longer levied there is a weight restriction of three tons after gales caused damage to the structure in 1976. The bridge was opened amidst great celebration in July 1831: construction of the new road gave access to Whorlton Village from a southerly direction for the first time. Below the bridge flat ledges of rock and deep pools among the waterfalls provide an ideal recreational setting during summer months, but the river has many hidden dangers and great care is called for on the part of those who set out to enjoy its attractions. Access to this section of the river bank—known as Whorlton Lido—is

Whorlton Bridge and adjacent toll cottage—completed 1829–31.

from an adjacent field and a charge is made for parking vehicles. Opposite the Lido the northern bank is almost vertical; during the Second World War this beautiful setting provided troops with an ideal venue for assault training.

Wycliffe

A footpath runs along the river bank into the tiny hamlet of Wycliffe, which lies little more than a mile downstream. Close to Wycliffe, a group of three buildings indicates the landing point for a ferry and the centre building was formerly an inn named "The Boot and Shoe". It was here that a number of patrons came to grief as they made their way from from the inn to the ferry in earlier times. A derelict boathouse is visible on the opposite bank and downstream from the ferry route a diagonal line of flat rocks marks a fording place. Running away from the river bank there are traces of the mill race that crosses a field towards the Mill House, formerly a sawmill and now restored as a private residence.

Wycliffe is the probable birthplace of one of England's foremost literary and

Wycliffe Church, which dates mainly from the thirteenth and fourteenth centuries, contains memorials to members of the Wycliffe family including the religious reformer John Wycliffe.

religious figures. John Wycliffe was born in 1320 at a time when his father was Lord of the Manor; though details of his early life are scarce he was born either at Wycliffe or nearby Hipswell. Educated by monks at Egglestone Abbey, he went to Oxford University at the age of fifteen and gained his master's degree five years later. After declining the living at Wycliffe, he became warden at Canterbury Hall, Oxford, in 1365 and here he published several pamphlets attacking the great wealth and abuses of the church. He clashed with the Pope over payment of an annual tribute, and supported the cause of the English peasantry before taking up the rectorship of Lutterworth near Rugby in 1370. John Wycliffe then trained a group of preachers who became known as "Lollards" or "Babblers" and spread a new concept of Christianity to the poorer classes. During the late thirteen-seventies he was twice accused of heresy and would probably have been condemned to death if it had not been for the intervention of powerful barons on one occasion and the London mob on the other. Wycliffe then spent three years translating the Bible into English, but he was blamed for instigating the Peasants' Revolt of 1381 and again accused of heresy. Finally his health gave way and he suffered a stroke and died on 31st December, 1384. John Wycliffe was buried at Lutterworth, and though his remains were dug up and ceremonially burned in 1428 the effects of his teachings were far-reaching. He had set in motion the moves that would be carried through by individuals such as Martin Luther and that culminated in the Reformation.

Much of Wycliffe church dates from the thirteenth century with some reconstruction work carried out in the following century. Fine medieval windows help to create an atmosphere of calm and beauty, with fragments of Saxon stonework and part of a hog-back gravestone recalling earlier buildings on the site. Members of the Wycliffe family are buried beneath the chancel with plaques and inscriptions providing biographical details. Wycliffe Hall dates largely from the early Georgian period, but there are traces of the earlier Elizabethan building at the rear. Large sections of the interior were destroyed by a fire in 1932, but Georgian plasterwork from places such as Halnaby Hall has been used to restore the building to its original state.

Wycliffe Hall, which was built in the early 1700s on the site of an Elizabethan mansion.

Ovington and Winston

A short distance away on high ground, the red-tiled cottages of Ovington cluster round a rectangular green. It gained fame as the "Maypole Village" and the Four Alls Inn displays a signboard representing the four callings:

The Queen	:	I govern all
A Soldier	:	I fight for all
A Parson	:	I pray for all
A Farmer	:	I pay for all.

Pleasant woodland lines both banks on the downstream stretch towards the impressive single span of Winston Bridge. Built in the early seventeen-sixties by Sir Thomas Robinson, it spreads some hundred feet across the Tees and was said to be the largest of its type in Europe. It was part of a network of roadways which carried coal to the riverside at Stockton for loading on to sea-going vessels, and it was one of few structures that remained intact after the disastrous flood of 1771.

The river is wide and fast-flowing in this final stretch of upland and the little village of Winston stretches along a ridge above steep tree-covered banks. Local folk have much to be proud of, for numbered among their ancestors are Thomas Wharton and Aaron Arrowsmith. Wharton was born in the village in 1614 and after studying at Oxford, Cambridge and London, he became physician to St Thomas' Hospital and Professor of Medicine at Gresham College. He is credited with the discovery of the duct of the submaxillary gland and made a special study of glands generally. Another famous local son, Aaron Arrowsmith, was baptized at Winston church in 1770 and after studying mathematics with William Emerson of Hurworth, he moved to London at the age of twenty. Soon he was producing large-scale maps of various parts of the world, including work for the East India and Hudson's Bay Companies. He died in London in 1823.

Winston church dominates the skyline at the eastern end of the village. A very wide, beautiful chancel from the thirteenth century also incorporates stonework from the Roman fort at Piercebridge. The font and nearby grave cover are also of thirteenth-century origin, but much of the exterior was rebuilt by John Dobson in 1848 in the early English style. Less than two miles downstream from Winston, there is an interesting contrast in fortunes. On the south bank little remains of the once-flourishing village of Barforth, but on the opposite bank there is the considerable style and elegance of Gainford.

Barforth and Gainford

Barforth is recorded in Domesday Book as "Bereford" and has also been known as "Old Richmond". The manor house still stands on flat ground close to the river, but apart from the ruined twelfth-century chapel of St Lawrence and a stone-built pigeon cote with some 300 nesting holes, there is little trace of the village. Elizabethan coins have been found in the vicinity, but stone was taken away long ago for walling and and there is no documentary evidence to explain the abandonment of this settlement.

Winston Church dominates a ridge above the Tees. Items of thirteenth-century masonry are built into the fabric, which was largely reconstructed in 1848 by John Dobson.

Across the river, Gainford provides a contrast and has a spacious green surrounded by red-tiled cottages with well cared for gardens and orchards. According to Symeon of Durham, Ecgred, Bishop of Lindisfarne from 830–845, built a church in the village; although the present church dates from the thirteenth century it contains stonework from much earlier periods. Fragments of Saxon crosses and stones from the Roman fort at Piercebridge, including an altar stone dated to AD 217, have been built into the north porch and tower. Church records date back to 1560; as well as drownings in the river, they also contain details of the constant battle to hold back the Tees as it erodes the churchyard. It has been suggested that the Northumbrian chief, Ida, was buried here in 801, and close to Gainford Hall a large field marks the probable site of an early castle. The hall was constructed between 1600 and 1603 by the Reverend John Cradock, but during the nineteenth century it became ruinous and extensive restoration was carried out. This tall, compact, stone building is designed to a double pile plan and it dominates the western end of the village. A circular dovecote in the garden provided a supply of meat during winter months and the structure, which is typical of a number of dovecotes in south west Durham, is listed Grade 2. The hall itself is Grade 1 listed.

Much of Gainford's elegance is due to its emergence as a spa resort during the late eighteenth century. The spa or "sulphurous spring" lies about three-quarters of a mile upstream from the village on the northern bank and can be reached along a riverside footpath. Since visitors came to Gainford to take the waters and stroll among the natural beauties of the area, housing was built around the green to provide holiday and retirement accommodation. There are a number of interesting buildings around the green and along the side lanes', most of them dating from the eighteenth century. The White House, built in 1712, was formerly St Colette's School, and the Mansion House dates from 1760. Gainford Academy is of a later period and an inscription "1818–1894" indicates its life as a school. Numbered among former pupils is Stan Laurel (one half of the Laurel and Hardy partnership); after recent restoration work the building stands proudly alongside the village's other imposing features. Recent housing development has spread along the northern side of the village around the Roman Catholic church of St Osmund. Opened in 1852 and built in the Early English style, it has an interesting interior. The north-western edge of the village lines up around the former railway station, now converted into a private residence, and by way of contrast the opposite end of Gainford is dominated by a complex of huge red-brick buildings. Opened in 1900 as a Roman Catholic Poor Law School, it was for many years St Peter's Community Home, but recent re-development and conversion work has provided nursing home accommodation and a range of units.

Piercebridge

Gainford's elegance was recognized in 1971 when the oldest part was designated a conservation area by Durham County Council; the nearby village of Piercebridge offers a dramatic insight into a much earlier period of occupation.

Gainford Hall dates from the early eighteenth century. A circular dovecote in the garden is typical of a number of such structures in south west Durham.

About two and a half miles downstream from Gainford, a Roman settlement developed around a river crossing point from about AD 70. It was in that year that Roman legions launched an attack on the nearby Brigantian stronghold at Stanwick and by the end of the century a supply route along Dere Street was well established. An agricultural community developed, along with a copper working industry and a vicus (civilian settlement) close to the permanent military presence, and although the early bridge was washed away in a flood during the middle part of the second century, this was soon replaced. A new fort was constructed in about 300 with strong outer defences enclosing about ten and a half acres; the present village of Piercebridge is built within these perimeter walls. The defensive wall was probably about five metres high with a wide cobbled berm outside and a large defensive inner ditch. This layout is visible in the section of the north-eastern corner, which has been excavated and consolidated. In 1933 a latrine building was discovered in the north-east corner of the fort, but the extent and importance of the Roman settlement was not appreciated until recent detailed excavations uncovered a range of buildings along the eastern side of the village. These remains have been consolidated and are open to the public with access from a lane alongside St Mary's Church, which dates from 1873. On the opposite side of the river, close to the former position of the vicus, the piers and abutments of the Roman bridge have also been exposed and consolidated for public viewing. The present course of the river lies a short distance away from these remains and an alternative theory was put forward by Raymond Selkirk suggesting that the stonework was, in fact, part of a canal system linked to the river. The existing bridge was constructed in the early sixteenth century, but a number of floods left its three pointed arches in a poor state of repair. Rebuilding work has restored it to its former glory. The importance of Piercebridge as a crossing point resulted in a skirmish during 1642, when Parliamentary cavalry under Fairfax was heavily defeated by Royalist forces. Skeletons of men and horses—casualties of this engagement— were unearthed during construction of the nearby railway last century.

The George Hotel occupies a prominent position between road and river on the line of Dere Street, and it is steeped in atmosphere. A female spectre is said to haunt an upstairs room and a grandfather clock on the ground floor serves as a reminder of the popular ballad "My Grandfather's Clock". The clock which . . . "stopped short, never to go again, when the old man died" recalls the fate of such a timepiece at the George Hotel on the death of a former landlord, Mr Christopher Charge.

Piercebridge is some forty miles from the source of the Tees and the river soon reaches lowland stretches, where it moves slowly serpentine loops south of Darlington.

Information for walkers

Below Barnard Castle there are rights of way on both river banks as far as Abbey Bridge. On the north side a clear path runs across the Demesnes to the road by the bridge while the alternative route crosses Thorngate Bridge and then runs to the left into East Lendings caravan park before emerging on the left of the hillside to turn eastwards. There are fine views of the impressive Bowes Museum from here and the route runs on into Abbey Lane passing Egglestone Abbey.

A riverside path runs for about a mile from Abbey Bridge on the southern bank. After crossing Manyfold Beck the path zigzags up the hill to cereal fields. Turning eastwards through more woodland, the path emerges in Mortham Lane by Rokeby Park and a left turn leads to the Meeting of the Waters.

The public footpath runs along the private road towards Mortham Tower. As the driveway curves right the footpath bears left to a stile and then crosses three pastures, runs through an open gateway with the wall on the right and then across a final field towards the road that runs to Whorlton Bridge. After crossing this bridge the route along the northern bank is waymarked to Winston Bridge, from where a footpath runs along the southern bank toward Barforth Hall. The next section of the route is privately owned and permission must be obtained in order to continue past the hall and across the wooden-planked bridge into Gainford. (There is no suitable footpath on the northern bank and the public road, A67, follows the river closely along this stretch.)

Beyond Gainford the footpath is sign-posted just east of the former St Peter's Community Home and a firm path follows the river bank downstream into Piercebridge.

Piercebridge has been an important crossing point since Roman times. The existing bridge largely dates from the early sixteenth century.

Dere Street, an important Roman thoroughfare, ran across the ground now occupied by the George Hotel at Piercebridge.

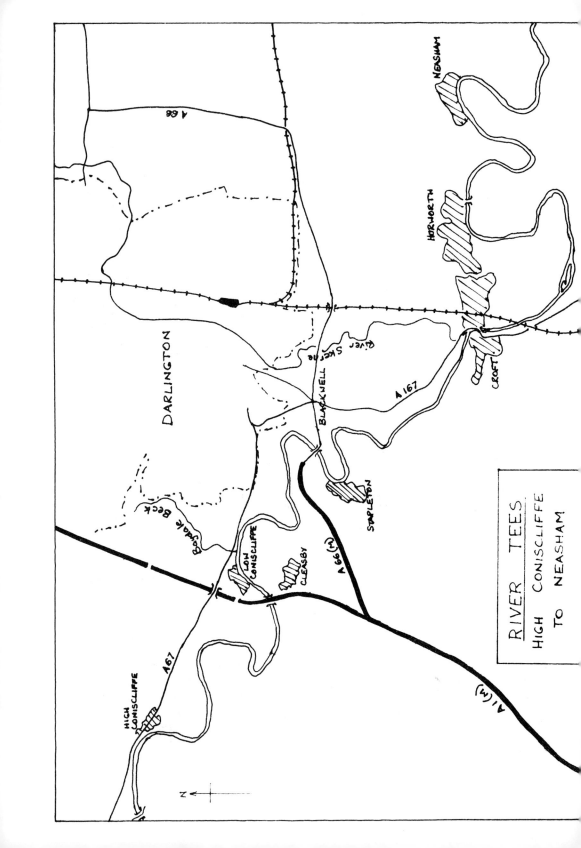

RIVER TEES
HIGH CONISCLIFFE
TO NEASHAM

CHAPTER FIVE

High Coniscliffe to Croft

HIGH Coniscliffe lies about a mile downstream from Piercebridge on a high river cliff alongside the A67 road from Darlington. There is mention of "Ciningesclif" in the Anglo-Saxon Chronicle (AD 778) as the place where a high sheriff named Eldulf was killed. The king at that time was Edwin of Northumbria and the church at High Coniscliffe is the only one in England to be dedicated to this early monarch. Several stones from the Saxon building on this site are built into the tower and outside fabric, but most of the present structure dates originally from the thirteenth century. Extensive restoration work in 1844 was followed by further remodelling in 1892, which included insertion of the clock.

The rocky spur around the church was extensively quarried during the eighteenth century, but these operations ended during the early eighteen-hundreds, leaving the former schoolroom, schoolmaster's house and vicarage isolated on a prominent outcrop. Local magnesian limestone and river boulders were widely used as building materials in the six farms and adjacent houses. During the nineteen-sixties two large farm buildings were demolished to make way for small houses, and the Methodist Chapel of 1826 was also replaced by housing. The Old Hall (No 23) probably dates from the late seventeenth or early eighteenth century, but most of the other properties were built in the late eighteenth or nineteenth centuries. Many of them have a roof with a wavy pantile construction.

High Coniscliffe Mill was one of three corn mills in the immediate locality—along with Carlbury Mill on the Tees and another on Ulnaby Beck. It is still possible to trace the dam and sluice gate at the rear of the building at the bottom of Mill Lane. A well-worn track leads from the roadside at High Coniscliffe down to the river bank and along to Low Coniscliffe. Across the river Holme House Farm is at the centre of gravel workings which characterize the river landscape between Piercebridge and Stapleton and there are clear examples of river terraces in this locality. In places erosion of the river bank has highlighted pebble beds covered with river silt.

At Low Coniscliffe the Baydale Beck joins the Tees and it is at this point that a modern bridge carries the A1(M) across the river. The Baydale Beck Inn stands alongside the A67 road across the fields from Low Coniscliffe. Local folklore describes it as the base for a notorious gang of thieves led by Sir William Browne, who was sentenced to death at Newcastle-upon-Tyne in 1743 after returning illegally from transportation. In those days this pleasant suburb of Darlington was said to be frequented by any number of law-breakers.

The small village of Cleasby lies south of the river, with buildings spread around a spacious village green. A memorial window in the church and a shield and mitre over the door of the old vicarage are permanent reminders of Cleasby's most famous son, John Robinson. He was born here in 1650, and during extensive overseas travels he became an important diplomat at the Swedish Court. On his return to this country he became Bishop of Bristol and Dean of Windsor. Despite his success John Robinson continued to pay regular visits to his birthplace, where he financed the building of the vicarage and school.

This western fringe of Darlington has a number of nurseries and market gardens, but it is the buildings of the Tees Cottage pumping station and its successor, the Broken Scar treatment works, that dominate the skyline on Coniscliffe Road. From 1849 a number of pumps were installed on premises situated south of the road to lift water from the Tees. After settlement, treatment and filtration, the water was delivered into Darlington, but as demand for water increased, further treatment capacity was established to the north of Coniscliffe Road. In 1926 a major expansion of installations was completed, but original machinery was retained as back-up. Modernization of the treatment plant brought an increase in capacity during 1955 and in 1972 another extension was added to the 13 million gallon per day plant. The water to feed the plant continued to be abstracted from the Tees adjacent to the site and the river level was maintained by discharging the required quantities into the Tees and its tributaries from the Northumbrian Water Board's reservoirs in Upper Teesdale. During 1980 original buildings at the Tees Cottage pumping station were threatenedd with demolition, but in November 1980 a charitable trust was formed to preserve buildings and equipment. Since then members have carried out restoration work on buildings and equipment, including the three pumping systems which were all the height of innovation in their time. The beam steam engine pumped more than four million gallons per day before being replaced in about 1914 by a gas engine. An electric pumping system of 1926 of equal rarity and some features of the pumping station are regularly opened to the public with both steam and gas engines in action.

A pathway runs from the Broken Scar Picnic Area down to the riverside, where some 500 tons of whinstone were strategically dumped during 1985 in order to reduce bank erosion.

Blackwell

Blackwell is a pleasant residential suburb on Darlington's south-western fringe which retains much of its former village atmosphere. Mature trees line many of the roads and a golfcourse, and the grounds of Blackwell Grange Moat House provide open aspects beyond the housing. Originally known as Blackwell Grange, this imposing mansion was, in 1736, the birthplace of George Allan. He was able to combine his work as a solicitor with an interest in genealogy, heraldry and natural history. In order to print and distribute his research work, Allan set up a printing press in his home, and after setting up his own museum and library at Blackwell Grange he invited other scholars to pay visits. On his death in 1800, his collection was bought by Newcastle Philosophical Society and formed the

Weir on the Tees at Broken Scar.

nucleus of displays at the Hancock Museum, where it remains to this day. Part is included in the Bewick collection and more material has been incorporated into the display concerning the voyages of Captain Cook. Blackwell Bridge was designed by John Green of Newcastle-upon-Tyne in 1832. Constructed of stone from Gatherley Moor, its three spreading arches have been widened on the south side and the old toll house still stands at the Yorkshire end.

Further along the Tees' northern bank and close to the confluence with the River Skerne at Oxen-le-fields, there are four great pools of water known as Hell's Kettles. Numerous legends are associated with these ponds, the largest of which measures one hundred feet in diameter: according to local folklore they appeared on Christmas Day, 1179, when the ground rose to a tremendous height and then fell "with an horrible noise". It is said that several local people died of fright that day, and ever since then strange happenings have been reported from the area of the pools. Screams and the neighing of horses are said to be linked with a farmer who defied local tradition and took a load of hay to Darlington Market on 11th June (St. Barnabas' Day), a day of rest. He is supposed to have disappeared as he passed the pools, snatched by the Devil

45

because of his impiety. Geologists offer a rational explanation for the pools by suggesting that a build-up of gases and water in large cavities in the magnesium limestone gradually worked through to the surface. Frogmen disproved myths which stated that the pools were bottomless and found that the deepest one was only twenty feet deep.

Croft

The village of Croft stands at an important bridging point, but this collection of imposing Georgian residences has many other points of interest. The stone bridge was built in about 1400 on the orders of Bishop Skirlaw. Its seven boldly ribbed and pointed arches were restored in 1673 and the road surface is now twice its original width. Down the years it has also been the setting for an interesting and unusual ceremony involving the Prince Bishops of Durham. The last Prince Bishop was Van Mildert and he took part in the ceremony on the centre of the bridge during 1826. This same ceremony took place in 1860 when Henry Montague Villiers was welcomed as Bishop of Durham. He travelled to

The impressive stonework of Croft Bridge dates in part from the early 1400s with restoration work in 1673.

the diocese by rail and the train stopped in the middle of the railway bridge over the Tees at Croft so that he could be presented with the falchion by a representative of the Lord of Sockburn. Proceedings involved presentation of the Conyers falchion to the Bishop by the Lords of the Manor of Sockburn. The Conyers Falchion is a broadsword which features in the story of the Sockburn Worm (see chapter six). It was presented to the Dean and Chapter of Durham in 1947—a gift from the last Lord of the Manor of Sockburn—and it is on display in Durham Cathedral. It was returned to the Lord of Sockburn along with wishes for good health and long enjoyment of the Manor.

The ceremony was revived on 20th September, 1984, when Dr David Jenkins was welcomed into his diocese by the Mayor of Darlington.

Quantities of red Triassic sandstone have been used in the construction of the bridge and nearby Croft church. Most of the church fabric dates from the fourteenth century, but there is Norman masonry in the west end and the tower is fifteenth century. Fragments of Saxon stonework, the handsome altar rails and restored screenwork round the south aisle chapel add to the building's interest, but the most astonishing feature is the Milbanke pew. It is about fifteen feet long and is supported on oak pillars with a stairway giving access from floor level. Byron and his bride are said to have sat here for Sunday morning service while spending their honeymoon at nearby Halnaby Hall, and Yorkshire's "Railway King", George Hudson, also worshipped here. He is said to have always turned his back on the parson when he sang, while his wife put up her parasol during the sermon. An ornate tomb dates from the seventeenth century and is a memorial to Sir Mark Milbank while another massive tomb has an inscription recording Sir Richard Clervaux's connections with Edward IV and Richard III. There are also reminders of young Charles Lutwidge Dodgson's early days at Croft, where his father was rector. He is better known as Lewis Carroll, author of *Alice in Wonderland*, and his family moved here in 1843 when he was eleven years old. Much of the inspiration for his early writings was gained in these surroundings as he converted the spacious rectory garden into a toy railway system with refreshment rooms, stations and a length of track. During structural alterations in 1950, a loose floorboard in the nursery of the former Dodgson home exposed items such as a thimble and a small white glove, which evoke memories of Alice, the Dodo and the White Rabbit. Croft became a very popular spa village during the nineteenth century. The old spa, now a farm building, dates from 1669, when Sir William Chaytor created a horse pond close to a sulphur well in order to treat two of his horses. Another spa was opened some three hundred yards from Croft Bridge in 1827 when Sir William's grandson built a pump room over the spring and then added a suite of baths. By 1837 some eight hundred clients were taking regular baths in the water from sulphur, magnesium and chalybeate springs. Chalybeate is a salt rich in iron. During the early nineteenth century, Croft's Spa Waters had become well known; they fetched a high price when sold in sealed jars in London. The Spa Hotel is mentioned in 1704 as a coaching inn serving travellers on the Great North Road. A new building had taken shape by 1808 as visitors flocked to Croft in search of the health-giving waters, and further extensive restoration work was carried out in 1973. By 1841 the number of people visiting the spas at Croft had declined considerably and today the only material signs of this boom time are the remains of walkways, wells and bridges in the neighbouring woodland.

The Bomber Command Station at Croft was opened in October, 1941, as a satellite to Middleton St George, and during the war years a whole range of aircraft were based there. These included Whitley MK Vs of 78 Squadron, Royal Air Force and Wellington MK IIIs of the Royal Canadian Air Force, and though the last Royal Canadian Air Force squadrons left in June, 1945, the base remained open until 1946. Since the war the airfield has been adapted to stage motor sports. Darlington and District Motor Club arranged events for two years starting in 1950 and during the mid-nineteen-fifties they organized sprint and speed trials for cars and motor cycles. These events attracted crowds of about a thousand, but facilities were limited until a consortium of local businessmen developed a 1.75 mile circuit in time for an inaugural meeting in August, 1964. TV Rallycross was launched at Croft, but plans to make it into a North East Grand Prix circuit did not materialize and the autodrome closed in October, 1981. Since then the circuit has staged rallycross events and motor-cycle training.

Information for walkers

There is a choice of routes between Piercebridge and Stapleton, but both involve sections of road walking.

A track runs east from the B6275 road which runs due south from Piercebridge. The path is quite well defined and offers fine views of the river near Cleasby. From Cleasby it is necessary to walk along the roadside footpath into Stapleton.

The alternative route runs along the northern bank. From Piercebridge a footpath leads to the A67 road at Carlbury and along the roadside into High Coniscliffe. A well-worn track runs from the road to the riverside below the settlement and follows the river to Low Coniscliffe. After rejoining the road close to the Broken Scar Treatment Works, a path runs through the picnic area back to the riverside and on into Blackwell, when it is again necessary to follow the road over Blackwell Bridge into Stapleton.

A lane runs from the south side of Stapleton to Stapleton Grange and then skirts south around Monk End Wood and into the yard of Monk End Farm at the western side of Croft. A humpback bridge near the farm yard is a reminder of the earlier importance of this bridle way between Croft and Stapleton.

Opposite page: Croft Church has links with Lewis Carroll, Lord Byron and George Hudson—"The Railway King".

Below: Croft Spa Hotel, popular with visitors who stayed in the village.

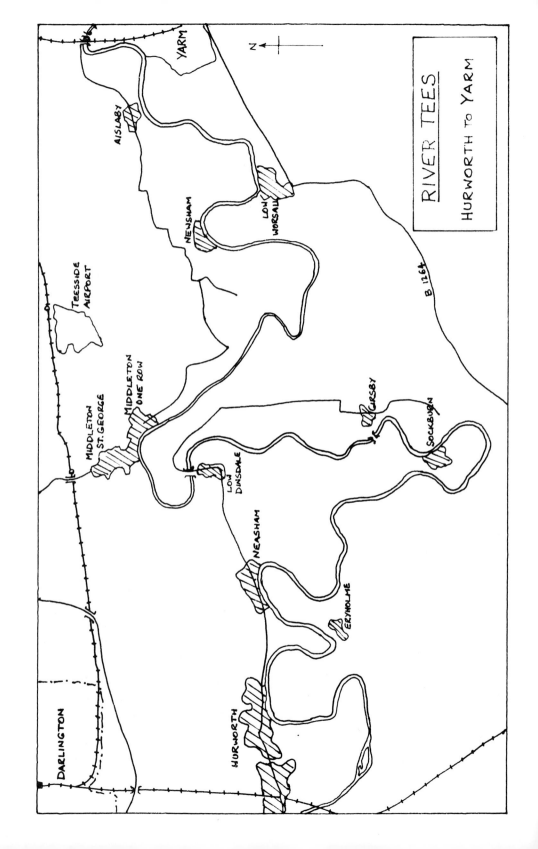

RIVER TEES

HURWORTH TO YARM

N

CHAPTER SIX

Hurworth to Aislaby

DOWNSTREAM from Croft, the river enters one of many lengthy meanders in this lowland section, but the public road follows a more direct route through Hurworth Place and on into Hurworth-on-Tees. This large, attractive village with elegant eighteenth-century buildings spreads along the north bank of the Tees on either side of a spacious green. During the last century Hurworth was noted for its linen industry and in 1830 120 hand-loom weavers were employed in premises situated mainly at the east end of the village. Today there is little sign of this early industrial activity and it is the architectural features of buildings around the green that provide a distinctive atmosphere. The attractive red brickwork, canted bays and pedimented door cases of buildings such as the Hurworth House Preparatory School and the Old Hall date from the eighteenth century and nearby cottage facades provide an interesting contrast.

Several buildings display firemarks indicating that the property was insured with a particular company, which would send its own engine and firemen if fire broke out, and a number of distinctive plaques highlight properties associated with William Emerson, an eccentric mathematician who was born at Hurworth in 1701. Emerson's early education was provided by his father—the village schoolmaster—and the local curate, and after furthering his studies at Newcastle and York, he spent a short time as a schoolmaster. William Emerson's fiery temperament was quite unsuitable for teaching; after abandoning his classroom, he journeyed to London in order to publish a series of mathematical manuals for beginners.

On his return to Hurworth, Emerson married the rector's niece and during the eighteen-forties published successful works entitled *Doctrine of Fluxions* and *Mechanics, Method of Increments*. He was a popular figure in the district and gained a widespread reputation as both a mathematician and a magician, but his behaviour and appearance became more and more eccentric. Dressed in homespun shirts—worn back to front—sleeveless waistcoat, untidy wig and old hat, he was blunt and abrupt in manner, yet local folk continued to seek his assistance in solving crimes and arranging mystical feats. In his later years, Emerson took up angling and would stand in the Tees for hours. He was offered membership of the Royal Society, but turned it down stating that he was damned if he was going to pay so much a year to have initials after his name when he had already burned so many farthing candles in writing his work. William Emerson died on 21st May, 1782, and is buried with his wife in Hurworth churchyard, close to the west end of the church tower. The church was almost entirely rebuilt during the nineteenth century, with only the nave pillars surviving from the medieval building. Effigies in arched recesses originate from nearby Neasham

Hurworth House Preparatory School, one of many mansions surrounding the village green.

Priory and the choir stalls are fashioned from oak that was salvaged when the rectory tithe barn was demolished in about 1880. Imaginative use of a partition created a "Church Centre" within the main body of the building in 1985 and a range of activities are held there during the week, in addition to the usual church services.

In earlier times the road between Hurworth and Neasham was said to be haunted by a headless hob, but in recent years the greatest danger has been from flooding as the Tees burst its banks. After serious flooding during the early days of 1982 improvements have been made to this section of the river bank.

Neasham Abbey, an early-nineteenth-century brick villa, stands close to the site of a Benedictine nunnery. Founded some time before 1156, it was dedicated to the Virgin Mary and had close links with the village of Sadberge, where several nuns were buried. A triangular shelter at the foot of Neasham Hill was originally a pumphouse dating from 1879 and from this point the river begins an eight mile-meander which encloses the fascinating remains at Sockburn.

*   *   *

The tomb of William Emerson, mathematician and magician, in Hurworth churchyard.

Sockburn

There is no remaining trace of the early village at Sockburn, but a complete hogback was found in the foundations of the chapel building during the late nineteenth century and experts believe that a major centre of Christianity flourished here before the Viking settlement. Hogback is the name given to grave covers or composite monuments. Ornate sides are topped by a ridge which curves slightly at either end. The Sockburn examples probably date to the tenth century. An ancient roadway ran down the length of the peninsula and across the Tees into Yorkshire until lengthy legal proceedings during 1867–69 resulted in the closure of the public highway.

The present Sockburn Hall was built by the Blackett family in 1834; the ruined chapel nearby creates an enthralling atmosphere of mystery and romance. Parts of the building date from the twelfth century and at one time it stood in the centre of a thriving community. Today there is little trace of the village of Sockburn in adjacent fields and the churchyard is overgrown and neglected, but a restored section of the chapel houses a collection of relics,

53

Sockburn Hall, built for the Blackett family in 1834, stands close to the ruined church and deserted village site at Sockburn.

including hogbacks, sections of stone crosses and medieval effigies. One of the effigies has been cited as that of Sir John Conyers. Though its style dates from before his time this noble knight is linked with Sockburn through the legend of the Sockburn Worm.

Many parts of the country have monster stories on a similar theme, with the neighbourhood terrorized by a dragon, "wyverne" or "worm" demanding daily supplies of food and milk or human sacrifices. Sir John Conyers is credited with putting an end to the frightful beast that terrorized the Sockburn district, and its final resting-place is said to be marked by a large limestone boulder in a nearby field. The falchion or broadsword which was used to slay the "worm" features in the ceremony on Croft Bridge involving newly-appointed Bishops of Durham, described in the last chapter. There are several possible explanations for these monster legends, including a large eel or river creature, but perhaps the most credible of these suggestions links the story with an invading Viking army and a confrontation between the local hero and the enemy chieftain. This section of the river has plenty of natural beauty but also an atmosphere of mystery and romance. Perhaps it was this enthralling scene that attracted William Wordsworth and his sister Dorothy to Sockburn on their return from Germany during the spring of 1799. They were guests of the Hutchinson family at Sockburn Farm and it was here that the poet fell in love with Mary Hutchinson. During his stay Wordsworth spent some time working on "The Prelude" and "The Poet's Epitaph". Coleridge also visited Sockburn at this time and it was not until December, 1799, that Wordsworth and his sister left for Dove Cottage at Grasmere. Three years later Mary Hutchinson joined him at Grasmere as his wife. The farm, hall and adjacent chapel are all on private land, but permission to view the chapel may be obtained by contacting the owner.

Girsby and Dinsdale

This sense of timelessness and tranquillity is also evident at Girsby, where a handful of cottages stand close to the tiny All Saints' church. Built in 1838 with a simple nave, bellcote and chancel, it has box pews giving space for sixty worshippers. A grassy track runs down from the village to the bridge that was provided by Mrs Theopilia Blackett as part of the settlement of the Sockburn Ford Dispute in 1869.

Low Dinsdale nestles in yet another bend of the Tees. The oldest building in the village is the Manor House, which has some thirteenth-century masonry. Soon after the Norman Conquest, the Surtees family moved into these parts and probably took their name from the location ("sur Tees"). They were probably responsible for the moats and feeder ditch that run towards the river from the area of the Manor. Much of the present Dinsdale Manor dates from the Tudor period and it may have been built by Christopher Place, who purchased the estate from the Surtees family in 1538. Francis Place was born at Dinsdale in 1647 and took up a career in law at Gray's Inn during October, 1663. He left London during the Great Plague of 1665 and turned to drawing and engraving, with the beautiful setting of St Mary's Abbey at York as his base. During his forty-year stay at York in the company of other artists, he experimented with pottery and specialized in portrait painting.

During 1799 William Wordsworth and his sister visited the Fish Lock Weir whilst staying at nearby Sockburn and at about the same time workmen uncovered a sulphurous spring as they bored through layers of whinstone in search of coal. Visitors were drawn to Dinsdale to take these healing waters and nearby another strong-smelling spring, known as the Leper's Bath, is said to have turned the bathers green. The Church of St John the Baptist was built in about 1196 on the site of an earlier Saxon church, but in 1876 the whole building was restored. A tower and vestry were added at this time and stained-glass windows in the south aisle also date from 1876. New pews, pulpit, font and lectern were installed and during 1901 a clock was incorporated into the tower. The lychgate was erected in 1908, but the church's red sandstone walls include a number of pre-Conquest fragments and inscriptions.

Until 1956 the toll-bridge that linked Low Dinsdale with Over Dinsdale was operated by the Over Dinsdale Estate of the Dodds and Williams families. The modern structure was put in place during 1956 on top of the earlier stone pillars and there are delightful views of the wooded river banks on both sides of the bridge. In recent years a number of artists and craftspeople have worked in this unspoiled natural setting and the river banks offer fine sport for angling clubs. A distinctive avenue of over a hundred lime trees line the roadside close to Over Dinsdale. They were planted in about 1907 at the same time as Over Dinsdale Hall was built; on the opposite bank of the river a pleasant pathway runs through woodland towards the village of Middleton One Row.

The Romans set up a bridging point a short distance upstream from the present settlement and a medieval castle covered the summit of Tower Hill overlooking the roadway ran northwards towards Sadberge. Modern housing now covers this site, but most of the village outline was established during the late eighteenth century.

During 1789 William Henry Lambton's workmen were prospecting for coal on his estate when they drilled into a sulphur spring. Earlier experience at Croft had ensured the spa's popularity and by 1797 this new spring had become popular for drinking and bathing. A cold bath was constructed, then a warm bath and a suite of dressing rooms. New baths were completed in 1824 and during the late eighteen-twenties much of Middleton One Row was updated to cater for the increasing numbers of visitors.

The opening of the Stockton to Darlington Railway in September, 1825, brought a constant stream of health-seeking travellers and during the late eighteen-twenties Lord Durham, son of Lord Lambton, built the large hotel on high ground above the bath-house. Design work was carried out by Ignatius Bonomi; the completed building had over seventy well-furnished apartments. Total costs amounted to about £30,000 and the range of facilities and stable block made it a fine venue for summer celebrations.

After only a few years, the Dinsdale Spa Hotel proved to be uneconomical and during the eighteen-fifties it became a centre "for a limited number of the higher and middle classes whose state of mind requires seclusion and medical treatment". In recent years it was operated as a Durham County Council Residential School and has now been converted into a nursing home for the elderly. It is known as Dinsdale Park Nursing Home.

Life was revolutionized in Middleton One Row during the early nineteenth century as first the spa and then the railway brought a range of tradespeople and services to the village. By the eighteen-twenties local directories included a butcher, grocer, innkeeper, tailor, shoemaker and blacksmith. Six years later there was a second butcher, a tea dealer, retailer of beer and a glover, along with two establishments where books could be brought or borrowed. An efficient postal service was provided for visitors and open-air bazaars were a further attraction. Closure of the spa and development of the Middleton Iron Works after 1864 brought quite different times to this beautiful hilltop setting that overlooks the Tees and the "Garden of Cleveland" on the opposite bank. In 1897 the local shipbuilding family, Ropners, opened a convalescent home for their

Opposite page: This avenue of trees at Over Dinsdale was planted in about 1907 at the same time as Over Dinsdale Hall was built.

workforce and for some twenty years, from 1908, the village doctor ran a sanatorium for tubercular cases in the grounds of his house.

The Church of St Laurence, which stands at the west end of the village, was opened in 1871 at a cost of £2,086 14s 4d. Before this time the only known place of worship in the parish was the tiny parish church of St George at the other end of the settlement. Parts of an early sundial have been built into the present structure—indicating probable Saxon origins—and later additions include the chancel, nave and porch. The building is mentioned in a document of 1291 and the decorated style of the arch suggests that it dates from the late thirteenth century. The building was re-roofed and extended in 1822.

The former wartime aerodrome of Goosepool straddles the Durham County–Cleveland boundary close to the church. Since 1966 it has operated as Teesside Airport.

Low Middleton Hall is situated on a delightful stretch of the river bank downstream from Middleton One Row. The original structure dates from the fifteenth century with a brick frontage added in 1720. Gardens lead to the Tees and the adjacent grounds hold a large octagonal pigeon house of red brickwork and tiled roof with over fifteen hundred individual cells. In earlier times the birds would supplement the winter food supply for residents of the Hall.

Newsham and Worsall

The deserted village site of Newsham overlooks the river between Low Middleton and Aislaby. Established in the late eleventh century, it was made up of between eighteen and twenty-five dwellings in 1309, when the population probably numbered about twenty. By 1390 one man owned the whole site, which indicates that depopulation had taken place during the fourteenth century. Aerial surveys have enabled historians to identify house sites, which would have had clay walls built on stone foundations and clay boundary walls in the gardens. A sunken road runs the full length of the village and leads down a steep bank to the river. The only remaining buildings are Newsham Hall, parts of which date from the seventeenth century, and the former chapel, which is now used by the local Women's Institute.

Worsall Wath marks the highest tidal point on the river; on the southern bank there are the remains of another deserted village site at High Worsall. This was named as "Wercesel" in the Domesday Book, when it was held by the King. It later passed to the Bishops of Durham and prospered as a busy market town during the sixteenth century. Today no building is left standing, apart from the ruined shell of St John's Church. Reconstructed with stone from an earlier building in 1719, it had seating for about fifty worshippers, but it was last used on a regular basis in 1894 and by 1910 served only as a mortuary chapel. The Reverend John Graves, author of *History and Antiquities of Cleveland*, is buried in the churchyard. Low Worsall was a small agricultural village until 1732 when Richard and Thomas Peirse began to develop port facilities. Construction of a stone quay and warehouses opened up an era of prosperity as merchandise from Swaledale and Teesdale, particularly wool and lead, was shipped out through

Peirsburgh or Peirsport. In spite of obstacles in the river between Worsall and Yarm, local farmers and tradesmen used this tiny port facility in preference to Yarm and materials were imported to enlarge the building that became known as Worsall Hall.

Worsall Hall dates from the eighteenth century, when the Peirse brothers settled in the village and began to develop shipping facilities on the nearby riverside.

Peirsport

The seventeen-fifties were the best years for trade at Peirsport; three round-bottomed boats, as well as a forty-ton sloop, *Cumberland*, were involved in coastal trade with Northern Europe and Scotland. Soon afterwards improvements were made to local roads and in 1764 work on Stockton's first bridge got under way—both factors which were to bring an end to river trade at Low Worsall. Stones from the quay were used to build a new church on the roadside in 1893 and during the nineteen-twenties the Tees Valley Water Board built a pumping station on the site of early port buildings.

Today the village has become a popular residential location with small pockets of modern housing added behind the original area of the green. Down the years this grassy expanse has provided a venue for a range of games, including golf, cricket and football, as well as sports meetings, Guy Fawkes Night bonfires and fishermen's gatherings. Worsall Hall is a reminder of busier times during the eighteenth century—Thomas Peirse lived there from 1730 to 1767 before moving to Acklam Hall. Among the secrets that it has given up are a mid-eighteenth-century mural illustrating the view from the Hall, discovered in 1929, and a brick-lined tunnel leading from the Hall's cellars to the river bank, discovered in 1959.

The pumphouse in Stobarts Lane was erected in about 1910, probably the work of the famous Scottish architect, Charles Rene Mackintosh. It was built in memory of Edward and Mary Temple, who were benefactors of the village and lived at nearby Saltergill Hall. Piersburgh Grange has had many uses over the last three hundred years. During the seventeenth century it was the Malt Kiln Inn, and when the village prospered as a port one front room served as a customs house. For the next two hundred years this large brick building was a farm, though it was used briefly as a school and also as a shop. By the late nineteen-sixties the building was badly run-down, but it has been carefully renovated to highlight an unusual chimney breast in the attic, an inglenook fireplace at ground floor level and a cellar which includes a barrel-vaulted roof and well in the middle of the floor.

Aislaby is a small village on the northern bank of the river close to Yarm. During the early part of this century there was an inn, the Black Bull, a smithy and a joiner's shop, but these premises are no longer in use and the main building that remains today is the Manor House Farm. The village green, known as the Slack, runs down to the river bank, where there was a landing stage for small vessels. Chalets line the downstream bank at Aislaby Lido and a pleasant walk leads through fields to Yarm Bridge.

Information for walkers

Leaving Croft Bridge and entering Hurworth Place, the road climbs steeply and on the right hand side a footpath sign directs walkers away from the road and across fields to a point where the footpath crosses the main east coast railway line. Extreme caution is needed at this point, but the path then enters the fields that are part of Rockliffe Park. At the end of this field section a stile leads on to a road, which runs away to the left into Hurworth.

The next part of the route involves walking along the roadside into Neasham and then on to Low Dinsdale, where a gate across the road from the church gives access to a field. The path then runs through woodland into Middleton One Row and on into Low Middleton, where it is necessary to return to the road before branching off along the track towards Newsham Grange.

At Newsham, the path returns to the river bank and follows the course of the river for the next few miles downstream to Yarm Bridge.

Opposite page: The Pump House at Low Worsall was erected in about 1910 and is probably the work of the Scottish architect Charles Rene Mackintosh.

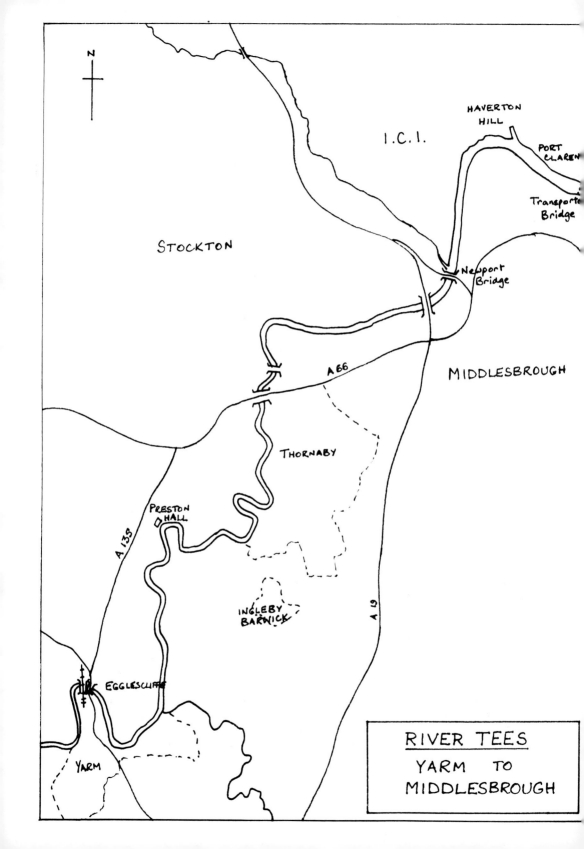

CHAPTER SEVEN

Yarm to Thornaby-on-Tees

T HE ORIGINAL settlement at Yarm lies within a large loop of the river on the route of the old drove road through Yorkshire and northwards across the Tees into Durham. This strategic position may have attracted settlers in the pre-Norman period—the township's name is derived from the old English "gearum" meaning fish pools—and it seems that Yarm was noted for its salmon fishery in Anglo-Saxon times. Down the years there were many name changes—the entry in Domesday Book of 1086 was "Larun" meaning a sheltered haven for mariners, and later variations include Yareham, Yareholme and Yarum. By the second half of the twelfth century a flourishing manorial borough with 135 burgages was involved in shipping trade with Scotland, Flanders and France. A section of grey stone walling alongside the modern Leven Road is the only surviving masonry from the hospital of St Nicholas established by Robert de Brus II in about 1130. The west end of the parish church is also said to date from the twelfth century and contains an unusual "fish" window—an almond-shaped slot in the wall of the tower. Much of the church was rebuilt in the pseudo-classical style following a fire in 1728. Among several features of interest within the building are the "Moses Window", probably installed by William Peckitt in 1768, which depicts Moses bringing the law down from Mount Sinai. There is also a splendid ornate Jacobean font.

Stone from the old hospital of St Nicholas was used to construct Yarm's first Grammar School, founded by Thomas Conyers on the south side of the churchyard in 1590. It overlooked West Street—for many years the town's main thoroughfare—which led to a fording point across the river. The existing road bridge dates from about 1400 and was built on the orders of Bishop Skirlaw of Durham. It replaced an earlier wooden structure at this point and until 1771 was the lowest crossing place on the river.

Down the years this fine stone bridge has taken a battering from traffic; its strategic importance was vividly illustrated in 1643 when opposing forces in the English Civil War fought a battle on land adjacent to its northern end. As traffic increased during the eighteenth century, plans were made for a replacement bridge built of iron. Work began in September, 1803, and the bridge was completed two years later, but before it could be brought into use the whole structure collapsed, on 12th January, 1806. Fortunately the old stone bridge was still intact and it was then decided to widen the roadway of this original structure. Ribbed arches of the early bridge are clearly visible from the river bank and from this point it is also possible to view the rounded northern arch. This section of the bridge was removed during the English Civil War—to be replaced by a drawbridge—and it was not rebuilt until 1785.

For about six hundred years—between the twelfth and eighteenth centuries—Yarm was the major port on the Tees. Sailing ships ranging from sixty to a hundred tons loaded exports of flour, wool, grain, hides, salt and lead at wharves that stretched from Silver Street downstream to the site of the skinnery on Atlas Wynd. Recent archaeological surveys failed to uncover evidence of these wharves and few of the adjacent grainstores and warehouses are still standing. Merchants and traders had houses built on the High Street and these help to give this broad cobbled roadway its interesting appearance. The Town Hall dates from 1710 and its Dutch style of construction illustrates the links between Yarm and the Low Countries at that time. Pantile roofs are a feature of many buildings along the High Street—shipped into Yarm by vessels returning from Holland. Plaques and tablets on buildings highlight events in Yarm's chequered history. Flood levels of 1771 and 1881 are marked on the Town Hall and several of the inns along the High Street have interesting associations. A group of local businessmen met in a room of the George and Dragon during February, 1820, to plan a railway linking the Durham coalfields with the Tees at Stockton. Towards the northern end of the High Street stands the Ketton Ox, a building that is over three centuries old, named after the famous shorthorn bred by Charles Colling of Ketton near Darlington in 1796. Reports of hauntings may be linked with the fact that a mortuary was once housed in the rear of the premises and with cockfights that were held in upper rooms after the sport had been banned in 1849. A secret flight of stairs provided an escape route from the cockpit room whenever officers of the law put in an appearance.

Tom Brown's House is no longer an inn, but memories endure of this local hero from the Battle of Dettingen in 1743 who charged into enemy ranks to recover the regimental standard. Dettingen is in Bavaria and the battle took place in the protracted War of the Austrian Succession, into which Britain had been drawn because of alliances. Its most notable feature is that it was the last time an English monarch, George III, personally led his army into action. On 8th June, 1969, a memorial stone was unveiled in Yarm churchyard by the Queen's Own Hussars, the modern counterpart of his regiment.

Memories of other notable individuals appear throughout Yarm. Benjamin Flounders, an educationalist, philanthropist and director of the Stockton and Darlington Railway, lived at Bridge House, and John Wesley established a strong Methodist following in the township. He is said to have visited Yarm on nineteen occasions between 1748 and 1788 and described the fascinating octagonal church of 1763 as "by far the most elegant in England". On the other side of the township stands Hope House. It dates from the early seventeenth century and is believed to be the oldest house in Yarm; a variety of building materials and architectural detail feature in its walls. A short distance away along West Street stands Yarm Castle. This cement model measures about two feet in height and dates from 1882, when a local builder, David Doughty, created a number of items to decorate the gardens of Commondale House.

Yarm is dominated by a 43-arch railway viaduct, extending the Leeds and Thirsk Railway from Northallerton to Stockton and Hartlepool. Construction work lasted from 1848 to 1852 and this gigantic enterprise produced a series of

Yarm Castle is a concrete model set on the wall adjoining Commondale House in West Street.

impressive statistics. The forty-three arches span 760 yards and include 7.5 million bricks and 139,000 cubic feet of stone. An army of navvies earned up to £1 each day during construction work. A stone tablet positioned in an arch above the river records the achievements of Thomas Grainger and John Bourne in designing the viaduct.

An annual three-day fair is held during October along the length of the High Street. Gypsy caravans, roundabouts, sideshows and stalls bring a special mix of noise, excitement and colour to the cobbled areas on either side of the Town Hall, but much of the earlier atmosphere has disappeared. During the closing years of the last century, the fair was of agricultural importance with a horse market on the first day featuring Cleveland Bays, with cattle sales taking pride of place on the second and sheep and cheese dominating the final day. After the Second World War sales of livestock were moved to the cattle mart and modern amusements began to dominate proceedings in the High Street.

The Blue Bell Inn which stands close to the northern end of Yarm Bridge was probably built in the first half of the last century. It became a popular stopping-off point for Irish cattle drovers herding their cattle to Yarm Fair and is said to be haunted by a former landlord, George Goldie. During his stay at the inn, Mr Goldie ensured a place for himself in local folklore by landing an eight-foot-long sturgeon in the eighteen-nineties and by his exploits as one of Yarm's last salmon fishermen during the early nineteen-hundreds.

65

Yarm viewed from the railway viaduct which spans the town. Until the late eighteenth century the road bridge at Yarm was the lowest crossing point on the Tees.

Egglescliffe

Egglescliffe church is situated on high ground across the river from Yarm. Parts of the nave date from the Norman period and the chancel was completed during the fifteenth century, but the church's most outstanding feature is its collection of wooden fittings. The carved chancel screen, choir stalls and panelling on the sanctuary walls all date from the Restoration period. Oak pews in the nave were also fashioned in the seventeenth century and the pulpit, reading desk and panelling in the side chapel are from the eighteenth century. Two chained books, Bishop Jewell's Apology and the Eikon Basilike, are displayed in this chapel and below them lies a stone figure showing a knight in armour with a winged dragon biting the bottom of his shield. It is thought to represent Thomas Aislaby, who fought at the Battle of Lewes in Sussex, and probably dates from the early fourteenth century.

Over the years the village green has been reduced in size, but careful reconstruction of the stone cross in 1984 has revived memories of the original layout. One of two village wells was situated on the lower side of the sloping green and wooden stocks stood a short distance to the south west of the cross while a corner of the southern side was for many years the location for the pound. The Old Hall was rebuilt in 1772 and is one of the few stone buildings in the village. Most cottages around the green are brick-built and in earlier times

Egglescliffe green retains its cross, but there is no sign of the stocks, well and quoits pitch that were also situated at the village centre.

several of them housed looms for weaving huckaback or blankets. The village was also well known for its gardens and orchards with Nicholson's garden on the south side of the green earning particular fame for its crops of strawberries.

Butts Lane is the main route into the village and its name is a link with the days when local menfolk had to practise their skills with crossbows on targets in an adjacent field. Surrounding the original Egglescliffe settlement is the spreading modern housing of Eaglescliffe. Reverend Isaac Basire, the local rector, is credited with using the name Eaglescliffe for the first time in 1619, but local tradition links the changed name with the railway age. The Stockton and Darlington Railway opened on 27th September, 1825, and when a station was built at nearby Preston Junction a sign writer is said to have been given a piece of paper with the incorrect spelling—Eaglescliffe—and the name has continued in use ever since.

In spite of the disruption brought by railway traffic, land between the tracks and river and Eaglescliffe was developed for housing during the later decades of the nineteenth century. Many of these properties covered large sites and had extensive gardens. They were often owned by local shipowners and industrial-ists, such as John Fowler, who played a major part in the development of the river. In 1854 he was appointed Chief Engineer to the Tees Conservancy Commissioners, the body responsible for operations on the Tees. The Tees Conservancy Commissioners were given control of operations on the river by

67

Act of Parliament in 1852. Before this time river business was in the hands of the Tees Navigation Company, which had offices at Thistle Green, Stockton. The TCC was replaced by the Tees and Hartlepool Port Authority on 1st January, 1967. With an annual income of about £4,000 and inherited debts of £80,000, the TCC faced serious financial problems; Fowler soon realized that prospects for the river would not improve until the river mouth was updated. A serious storm during February, 1861, brought further losses of shipping off Tees Bay and John Fowler drew up plans for breakwaters on either side of the river estuary. These are fully described in chapter ten. He became a leading authority on river development and was consulted about plans for many British river systems, including the Humber, Trent, Mersey, Clyde and Shannon, as well as similar projects in France and Spain. In 1868 he moved into a newly-built residence at Eaglescliffe. The house itself included a conservatory and decorative hothouse while adjoining gardens were stocked with rare trees and shrubs.

Preston-on-Tees

Preston-on-Tees is mentioned in the Boldon Book of 1183, but although land in the district was in continuous agricultural use after that time, no major buildings were erected until 1825, when David Burton Fowler gave orders for construction of the Hall on a site overlooking the Tees. Extensive grounds surrounded the Hall on the northern side, although the view was spoiled for a number of years by locomotives travelling along the line of the Stockton to Darlington Railway on an embankment which ran parallel with the main road from Yarm to Stockton. The Leeds Northern opened in 1852 with lines on the west side of the A19 road, while the Stockton–Darlington lines ran on the east side. Stockton––Darlington traffic was moved to the Leeds Northern tracks on 25th January, 1853, and Eaglescliffe became an important rail junction from this time. In 1882 the estate was purchased by Sir Robert Ropner, a local shipbuilder, and he modernized and extended the Hall. The Ropner family continued to live at Preston Hall until 1937 when it was put to use as office accommodation. After the Second World War the building became empty, and demolition was considered until Stockton Borough Council purchased the Hall and parkland for public use. Preston Hall was opened as a museum in 1953; in recent years it has become one of the north of England's major attractions. Galleries within the main building house displays of pewter, including items of Stockton ware by Edmund Harvey, a collection of arms and armour, snuff boxes and children's toys. Aspects of Victorian life have been recreated in a series of rooms on the first floor, and a full street of nineteenth-century shops provides a genuine glimpse of local life during the Victorian era.

Opposite page. Above: Preston Hall was constructed in 1825 on a site overlooking the Tees and with fine views in a southerly direction towards the Cleveland Hills.

Below: Looking upriver towards Yarm from the river bank close to Preston Hall.

During 1968 a number of paintings were discovered at Preston Hall. These included works by Lowry and Turner, but the most outstanding item was a masterpiece by Georges de la Tour. *The Dice Players* is a superb example of this artist's work and is now on display at the museum. Born at Vic-sur-Sielle in Lorraine, France, in 1593, Georges de la Tour moved to Luneville in 1620, where he became established as a master painter. In 1639 he was appointed Painter in Ordinary to Louis XIII and his successful career continued up to his death in 1652. *The Dice Players* is one of his later paintings and illustrates his fascination with the effects of light. Only 32 of his works are still known to be in existence and the only other example of his work to be found in this country is in the Queen's Collection at Hampton Court.

Grounds which surround the Hall provide a variety of activities, including woodland walks, a children's play area and two nine-hole golf courses. The skyline above the river is dominated by a large aviary with a dome-shaped roof. Former quarry workings in nearby woodland have been landscaped for public access with walkways and ponds. Whinstone was quarried from this vein, which runs across the river to Ingleby Barwick, and materials were shipped away by river for use in road-making.

Ingleby Barwick and Thornaby

Several sites of archaeological importance have recently been identified at Ingleby Barwick. These include a possible Romano-British settlement adjacent to Quarry Farm, medieval settlements at Cold Ingleby and Barwick and a motte and bailey castle which lies close to the confluence of the Rivers Leven and Tees. Other buildings of interest are widely dispersed throughout this area. Most of them are attractive Georgian farmhouses and outbuildings, dating from the mid-eighteenth century to the late nineteenth century and constructed with red hand-made bricks and clay pantiles. During the nineteen-sixties plans were made for extensive housing development at Ingleby Barwick and the scheme received approval from the Secretary of State in 1978. Original plans allowed for seven "villages" with a total of ten thousand homes by the year 2010, but by the mid-nineteen-eighties development had slowed down and fallen behind schedule. As the new settlement took shape, efforts were made to retain rural features of Cleveland and North Yorkshire with careful use of building materials, such as pantiles and yellow sandstone blocks. Development at Ingleby Barwick is taking place close to the spreading township of Thornaby. The original settlement grew up around St Peter's Church, which still stands on the green, and although Thornaby is mentioned in the Domesday Book of 1086, the church is not listed. It was one of the churches given by Robert de Brus to the recently established priory at Guisborough during the twelfth century and by 1539 when King Henry VIII's commissioners closed church buildings, the lands at Thornaby had considerable value with fifty-seven tenants of the priory listed on a rent roll. After the Dissolution, ownership of Thornaby manor and church was removed from Guisborough Priory and between the sixteenth and eighteenth centuries the church was a chapel of ease within Stainton parish.

Much of the existing building probably dates from the twelfth century and its most interesting internal feature is the chancel arch which includes both Norman and Early English work. The churchyard was closed in 1870 and during 1970 the boundary hedge was removed to give all-round views of the green. Sundial House is situated at the southern end of the green and an inscription on the sundial includes the date 1621—indicating the building's original date of construction. Most of the other properties around the green date from this century, but there is an atmosphere of timelessness around the little church, with ridges and hollows in the turf providing interesting talking points.

The tiny church of St Peter stands on Thornaby Green at the centre of the original settlement.

In 1825 William Smith of Stockton opened a pottery works on riverside land about half-a-mile downstream from the village. Skilled workers were recruited from Staffordshire and warehouses were opened in Rotterdam, Hamburg and Belgium as the brown pottery and ornamental items were exported from Thornaby. During 1838 further expansion took place close to the road bridge as William Smith built workers' cottages and shops. One of the north of England's first cotton mills was opened during the following year and the new community of South Stockton expanded rapidly as timber yards, ship and boat building yards and a general foundry were built within the curve of the river. By 1892 some 1,800 men were employed at the shipyards of Richardson Duck and Company and Craig Taylor and Company, and in the same year the red-brick town hall was opened at a cost of £7,000. The focal point for this industrial

71

community was a large standard which supported five gas lamps. Known locally as the Five Lamps, this distinctive structure included a drinking fountain and was the gift of three local Justices of the Peace. On 6th October, 1892, the Municipal Borough of Thornaby was formed by amalgamating South Stockton and the old village of Thornaby, with a total population of 15,637. Poverty and hardship was particularly severe in Thornaby during periods of industrial depression, but a strong community spirit developed within this close-knit settlement along the southern bank of the Tees.

During the last thirty years there have been major changes in the Thornaby area. In 1962 Thornaby Town Council acquired 347 acres of land adjacent to the former RAF airfield and work began on a new town centre. The first stage of this development was completed in 1967 at a cost of approximately £4 million and in the same year English Industrial Estate Corporation began work on an industrial estate for the Board of Trade. Since then light industrial units have been developed on 350 acres of land, which was part of the former wartime airfield. At Thornaby the river enters its final phase, with industrial and housing development lining both banks. From this point the water course has been adapted to meet the needs of shipping and land-based industries. In 1810 a channel measuring 220 yards was cut across the neck of a loop that ran close to the village of Mandale. The only building that remains from these earlier days is Mandale House, which incorporates the original three-hundred-year-old dwelling and adjacent Georgian inn.

Land within the loop of the original river channel—Mandale Bottoms—was until recently the venue for Stockton Racecourse, but a large shopping and leisure complex is being constructed on this low-lying ground. A sector of land close to Victoria Bridge, formerly the site of Head Wrightson's Teesdale Works, has been cleared and is also being redeveloped by the Teesside Development Corporation with housing and commercial premises.

Information for walkers

A riverside footpath runs along both sides of the township of Yarm (and copies of a local guidebook and trail are available in bookshops and newsagents along the High Street). From the northern side of the road bridge a footpath leads downstream below the village of Egglescliffe and around a bend in the river before turning away from the river bank to link up with the main road between Yarm and Stockton.

Quarry Road at the western edge of Preston Park runs into woodland close to the river bank; from here there is a pleasant walk along the river's edge below Preston Hall. The woodland walkway turns uphill and then veers to the right through a gate and across grassland to link up with the road to Stockton.

Near to the river it is possible to pass under the Surtees Bridge, which carries the A66 across the Tees, and walk into Stockton or cross via a walkway on the bridge into Thornaby. There are pleasant riverside walks on both banks upstream from the Surtees Bridge, but there is no continuous access on either side into Yarm.

CHAPTER EIGHT

Stockton-on-Tees to Middlesbrough

THE River Tees has played an important part in shaping Stockton's development. During the tenth century an Anglo-Saxon estate centred around nearby Norton was given to the Bishop of Durham by a son of the Earl of Northumberland. Much of the original crossing tower and north transept in St Mary's Church dates from that period and the parish of Norton, which covered approximately fifteen square miles along the north bank of the Tees, included Stockton along with several other small settlements. The first documentary reference to Stockton appears in the Boldon Book of 1183—the Palatinate of Durham's equivalent of Domesday Book. The survey revealed that Stockton had a hall which was used by the Bishop during his tour of the diocese and in 1189 Bishop Pudsey purchased the manor of Stockton, along with the royal manor of Sadberge.

During the thirteenth century the township of Stockton was developed by the Bishops of Durham to compete with Yarm and Hartlepool. Considerable growth in shipping and general business brought an increase in population and the Bishop's Manor House, which covered a large riverside site at the southern end of what is now the High Street, was rebuilt and restyled. Scottish raids during the fourteenth century and a destructive fire in 1597 resulted in further rebuilding work, but the castle's final demise came during the English Civil War. Royalists garrisoned the buildings in the early stages of the war until Scottish forces took over in 1644. When Parliament met in October, 1645, it was decided to dispose of castle lands and materials, and following clearance of the site in 1652 much of the stonework was re-used for building schemes in the town.

By the mid-eighteenth century, Stockton had become a thriving Hanoverian township. The new parish of Stockton was founded in 1713 and the fine church that occupies a site at the northern end of the High Street shows the guiding influence of Sir Christopher Wren. A red brick exterior encloses many features of interest within the main body of the church. Galleries which were added in 1719, 1748 and 1827 made the interior much darker and were removed during the eighteen-nineties, along with box pews. At about this time the fine triple-decker pulpit was reduced to a double-decker and moved from its central position. A chancel was added as part of an Edwardian scheme of improvements and in 1925 a side or lady chapel was built on to the south nave aisle. Another extensive restoration scheme was completed during the early nineteen-eighties and a service of rededication was held on 11th June, 1984. A series of finely-carved pew ends recall people and events from the town's past and the superb acoustics of the church have been utilized in recent years for musical performances.

The first mention of the Mayor's House at Stockton is made in Hatfield's Survey of 1384, but the present building dates from 1735. This distinctive Dutch-style structure was partially reconstructed some nine years later with the addition of an inn, cellars and four bow-fronted shops. Down the years it has been the setting for a number of famous events. On 18th September, 1810, over seventy guests celebrated the opening of the cut in the River Tees between Portrack and Stockton. There was more merrymaking in 1825 as the Stockton and Darlington Railway was opened, but the most spectacular reception was reserved for a visit by the Duke of Wellington on 24th September, 1827, when the centre of the town was swathed in decorations.

Close to the Town House stands a Doric column erected by John Short in 1768 at a cost of £45 and a few yards further south is the Shambles, which dates from 1825 and represents the third such building on this site.

Since the nineteen-sixties this central section of Stockton's wide high street has been the setting for the town's twice-weekly market. Other sectors of land close to the town centre were used previously and market charters were granted in 1310, 1602 and 1665. Stockton's increasing importance as a business and commercial centre during the eighteenth century provided a number of eminent characters from all walks of life. Joseph Reed supplemented his income from a rope-making business by writing poetry and plays. Some of his early works were badly received by the critics, but a farce, *The Register Office*, enjoyed a good run at the Drury Lane Theatre, London, in 1761 and his comic opera, *Tom Jones*, also enjoyed a measure of success. Joseph Ritson established a conveyancing business in the Stockton area before moving to London to be a conveyancer at Gray's Inn. Brass Crosby also left his home town for the capital, serving as councillor, sheriff and alderman before his election as Lord Mayor of London in September, 1770.

Prominent among a strong Baptist following in Stockton was Thomas Sheraton. Born in 1751, he began work as a journeyman cabinet-maker with a local timber firm. His skill as an artist and draughtsman was soon appreciated, but there were few outlets for his work in the North East and in about 1790 Sheraton moved his family to London. Years of over-work followed and he died in October, 1806. It was some forty years later that the importance of his design work began to be fully appreciated.

Another of Stockton's famous sons was born on 29th May, 1781, at 104 High Street. John Walker spent his early years in Stockton before moving to Durham and London to complete his studies as a surgeon. On his return to Stockton, he set up as a druggist at 59 High Street and after experimenting for years to discover a means of igniting a suitable compound by single friction he made the break-through in 1826. During that year John Walker produced a flame on three inch splints which had been dipped in a chemical mixture; by 23rd September, 1829, sales of 23,206 friction lights had been recorded in his day book. In February, 1858, he retired from business and moved to a house overlooking the green behind the parish church. He died there in May, 1859, without bothering to patent his dramatic invention.

During the late eighteenth and early nineteenth centuries, Stockton gained in importance as a shipbuilding centre, and local yards built vessels for the Royal and Merchant navies as well as a large number of colliers. A number of associated trades supplied materials such as linen, cloth, sailcloth, ropes and shipfittings. This expansion continued during the nineteenth century until the late eighteen-hundreds saw shipbuilding enterprises move down river to the booming development on the riverside at Middlesbrough.

Until 1911 Stockton remained the lowest bridging point on the Tees. Victoria Bridge was opened in 1887 to replace an earlier five-arched structure of 1769 and a short distance upstream the original railway suspension bridge of 1830 was soon replaced by a more durable steel bridge. The High Street area changed considerably during the nineteenth century. Almshouses built on an island site at the south west end in 1662 were demolished in 1816 and replaced by a new building, which contained a dispensary and a penny bank. This building, in turn, was demolished in 1896 and the impressive Victoria Buildings were erected on the site during the closing years of the last century. A number of coaching inns were included in the south-eastern section of the High Street and carrier services linked these premises with other market centres in North Yorkshire and County Durham. On the opposite side of the High Street stood the Borough Hall. Built in 1852, it was one of the best-furnished entertainment venues in the North of England, with a main hall and balcony giving a total capacity for seven hundred people.

Three graceful arches of Victoria Bridge link Stockton with Thornaby. Opened in 1887, the bridge replaced an earlier one dating from 1769.

The nineteen-seventies and nineteen-eighties have seen dramatic changes in Stockton's central lay-out. The parish church, Town House and Shambles building remain as reminders of the town's emergence as a market and business centre, but the south-eastern section of the High Street has been replaced by a modern shopping complex, the Castle Centre. The last vessel left Stockton's Corporation Quay in August, 1967, and the sector of land that was covered by a railway line, warehousing and riverside taverns has been redeveloped with a dual carriageway road and riverside footpath. An area behind the parish church—Thistle Green—was also cleared of housing and is now covered by the town's police station and award-winning library.

Stockton riverside was re-developed in the early 1970s with commercial and business premises as well as a new road system.

Portrack and Newport Bridge

Downstream from central Stockton there are few reminders of the shipyards and engineering works that lined both banks until the late nineteen-eighties. On the northern bank a large sector of land was covered by the Malleable works of the South Durham Steel and Iron Company, but only a small section of this plant remains in operation as the British Steel Stockton Works. The Stockton Malleable Iron Company set up works at Portrack in 1862. Steel smelting facilities were extended during the eighteen-eighties and eighteen-nineties with a total workforce of over two thousand. Amalgamation with other local steel and iron companies in 1898 led to the establishment of the South Durham Steel and Iron Company. During the nineteen-eighties industrial eyesores have given way to gently sloping areas of grassland under Cleveland County Council's schemes for reclaiming and improving former industrial sites. As part of this programme a riverside footpath has been created between Stockton and Newport Bridge. Plant and animal life has returned to sectors of land alongside the river, and development of Portrack Marshes as a wildlife reserve has provided a habitat for a range of insects and birds. In 1831 a cut was completed in the course of the river at Portrack so that a channel measuring 1,100 yards long and 75 yards wide replaced the tortuous meander. Much of the original river channel has been filled in, though it is still possible to pick out its starting point. The change in the course of the river led to the decline of shipping business at Portrack. During the late eighteenth century there was a considerable trade in whale oil and vessels called regularly with cargoes from Greenland. Shifting sandbanks often posed problems for sea-going craft; gangs of men were hired to drag or "rack" the ships round bends in the river at Portrack. Workers could slake their thirst in a nearby tavern known locally as the Flaming Stump and this building included the Angel Room with walls displaying a pattern of foliage and cherubs on a deep frieze. During the late nineteen-fifties unsuccessful efforts were made to preserve parts of this fine structure; it was demolished shortly afterwards.

Teesside Development Corporation has drawn up plans to construct a barrage across the Tees at Portrack, and the Bill to authorize such a scheme is under political discussion at the moment. Completion of a barrage would maintain a constant water level at Stockton and other locations further upstream so allowing greater use of the river for recreational and sporting activities. On the southern bank of the river British Rail's Motive Power Depot and Sidings cover the strip of land between Thornaby and the Tees (Newport) Bridge. The Tees Viaduct—opened in November, 1975—carries the A19 road across the river. It has some two hundred moving parts and individual joists to allow expansion and contraction, and an eighteen-inch-deep deck is locked on to girders which feature prominently in the structure. During March, 1988, it was calculated that 40,000 vehicles crossed the bridge daily, but strong winds have often caused temporary closure of both carriageways.

Low-lying land on the northern bank between the A19 and Newport Bridge approach road is covered by the Portrack sewage treatment works. This plant, which became operational in August, 1983, covers 40 acres of land and provides primary treatment for about 60 million gallons of sewage a day from the Stockton, Thornaby and Eaglescliffe area. It represented the first step by the Northumbrian Water Authority to clean up the river estuary of domestic and industrial filth.

Newport Lift Bridge, opened on 28th February, 1934, by His Royal Highness, the Duke of York, was the first vertical lift bridge to be built in this country and was the heaviest of its type in the world. Design work was done by Mott, Hay and Anderson and the structure was built by Dorman Long. In order to allow shipping to pass along the river, the bridge was designed to lift vertically over its centre span. This operation was carried out by passing ropes through sheaves at the four corner towers to give headroom for vessels of up to 125 feet (depending on the state of tides). Two 325 hp motors provided the power to lift the central road section and the whole operation could be completed in approximately one and a half minutes. An average of 800 vessels per week passed under the bridge until recent years (with the peak time during the inter-war period producing a record 1,400 lifts in one week), but during summer 1989 a Bill passed through Parliament to allow the bolting down of the bridge in order to save maintenance and replacement costs. On the northern approach to the Newport Bridge—the A1130—traffic crosses the Billingham Branch Line Bridge. Designed by Sir Gilbert Roberts, the five-spanned 226-foot bridge was

Newport Lift Bridge, opened on 28th February 1934, was this country's first vertical lift bridge and the heaviest of its type in the world.

the country's first welded bridge and represented a major step in bridge construction by using techniques since copied in many later bridges.

Downstream from Newport Bridge on the northern bank much of the land is covered by ICI Billingham Works. Vessels still call at the ICI Billingham Reach Wharf and ICI Bamlet's Wharf, but sectors of the river landscape are constantly changing as old traditional industries, such as shipbuilding, are replaced by aspects of the offshore industry.

The former Furness Shipyard at Haverton Hill, which closed in spring, 1979, is now run by British Shipbuilders Property Services. Slipways remain as a reminder of the great shipbuilding days, but the impressive headquarters building and nearby model village have been demolished. The yard was built during 1917 on eighty-five acres of low-lying land, with much of the construction work done by women, ex-servicemen and Irish navvies. A steamer of 10,000 tons was the first vessel to be launched at the yard—in 1919—and in the final years before closure supertankers were built here by Swan Hunter Shipbuilders Ltd. Workers were housed in an attractive estate built by the Furness Company, but encroaching industrial complexes produced an intolerable level of pollution and the whole village was cleared. Sections of unused roads are all that remain of the site and it has now reverted to grassland. A curve in the river channel below Newport Bridge encloses some ninety-eight acres of land which until recent

Cherry Bee, a vessel involved in trans-shipment on the Tees, was taken out of service in 1986. North Tees Power Station buildings in the background were demolished during the early months of 1990.

years was known as the Ironmasters' District. During the late nineteenth century local industrialists had built blast furnaces, furnaces and rolling mills on this low-lying ground. Several of these businesses were taken over in later years by Dorman Long and the longest-operating blast furnace plant was the Ayresome Ironworks, which continued in use from 1872 to 1965. The postwar years saw the decline of industry on this site and during the nineteen-seventies most of the area was reclaimed as grassland with a pleasant riverside walkway. A former slag heap was landscaped as a recreation area—Teessaurus Park—complete with a family of metal monsters. Teessaurus Park, which covers twelve acres of the Riverside Park industrial estate, was officially opened by the Mayor of Middlesbrough, Councillor Charles Godfrey, on 17th June, 1982. Adjacent land was developed during the early nineteen-eighties as the Riverside Park Industrial Estate and in November, 1983, it was announced that an area covering about 190 acres had been designated as the Britannia Enterprise Zone. A range of factories, sites and workshops were soon established, along with an Ocean Technology Site and Cadcam Technology Centre. Much of the river frontage on both banks from this point is dominated by assembly yards associated with the offshore industry. Sheds at Redpath Offshore's Linthorpe Dinsdale module yard on the edge of the Enterprise Zone cost £8 million. They were built to allow work on two floating hotels for the Marathon Oil Brae B Project to continue unhindered during severe weather.

Middlesbrough

Today Middlesbrough occupies a central position in the sprawling conurbation that covers low-lying land on both banks of the River Tees. High-rise office accommodation and large shopping complexes dominate much of the central sector with wide straight roads radiating in all directions. Yet in 1801 the small farming hamlet on this land had only four houses and twenty-five inhabitants and by 1829 there were still only forty inhabitants. Middlesbrough's rapid development during the remainder of the nineteenth century was unequalled by any other British settlement. At the census of 1831 the population had risen to 154 and in 1841 to 5,463. These ten years mark the planned development of the community by the "Middlesbrough Owners" as a port for the shipment of coal at the terminus of the Stockton and Darlington Railway. The rail link from Stockton to Middlesbrough was opened in 1830, and under Joseph Pease and other Darlington-based Quakers plans were drawn up to develop some five hundred acres of salt marshes as a major port. A "new town" was laid out behind the coal staithes on a grid-iron pattern around the central square. North Street, South Street, East Street and West Street ran at right angles from the central square and the parish church of St Hilda.

During the eighteen-forties the developing township gained a range of

Opposite page: Fire tug and fire-fighting vessel berthed near the Transporter Bridge.

urban institutions, including Methodist chapels, a Mechanics Institute, school buildings and a town hall. Workers arrived in Middlesbrough from all parts of the country and the population rose from 7,431 in 1851 to 19,416 in 1861 and 39,563 in 1871. From the eighteen-fifties Middlesbrough's industrial base was dominated by iron-making as Henry Bolckow and John Vaughan exploited deposits of iron ore in the Cleveland Hills. By 1873 the north eastern ironfield, with Middlesbrough at its heart, was producing over two million tons of pig iron—about one third of total British output. Bolckow played a major part in Middlesbrough's development as the town's first Mayor, first Member of Parliament and major benefactor. He laid the foundation stone of the town's Exchange Building in 1866 on a site to the south of the original township and other municipal and commercial premises were built in this sector of land. A new Town Hall was opened in 1887 and the splendid Empire Theatre was opened alongside in 1899. During the twentieth century Middlesbrough has continued to move southwards. Housing development spread between the main roads that linked Middlesbrough with the small settlements of Linthorpe, Acklam and Marton. As traditional industries, such as shipbuilding and iron-making, declined in importance, ICI Ltd provided much-needed employment for the local workforce with new chemical complexes on the northern bank of the river at Billingham (in the nineteen-twenties) and at Wilton on the south side (during the post-war years).

Since the early nineteen-seventies much of central Middlesbrough has been re-developed and there is little to see of the original layout of the Victorian new town beyond the railway line that runs to nearby coastal towns. Middlesbrough's northern skyline is dominated by the Transporter Bridge. Opened on 17th October, 1911, by HRH Prince Arthur of Connaught, this amazing structure carries a suspended car across the Tees and provides an important cross-river link. Down the years it has suffered several alarming incidents. In 1919 a three-masted Norwegian vessel had its mast carried away while passing under the bridge and during the Second World War a German bomb dropped through the girders and exploded on the empty car deck. In 1953 the bridge's winding gear broke down during gales and the car was stranded in mid-river for forty-five minutes as waves lapped around the "deck". Collisions and near-misses with river craft mark the bridge's recent history, but after extensive maintenance and repair work during the nineteen-seventies its future seems assured.

A rail link to Port Clarence allowed coal shipments from the north bank to begin in 1834—in direct competition with the Stockton to Darlington line across the river. Iron and glass works were opened on adjacent land and the opening of the Losh Bell and Company ironworks in 1853 brought a major influx of workers and their families. A new community grew up in the shadow of the extensive works and Bell Brothers (who took over the Losh Bell Company) provided a school for local children, followed by employment in their foundries for boys of school-leaving age.

The discovery of a layer of rock salt at a depth of 1,127 feet in 1874 was not exploited until 1882, when Bell Brothers developed a method of extraction. During the eighteen-eighties experienced salt workers were brought from

Cheshire and housed at nearby Haverton Hill. Extensive salt workings covered the coastal strip that runs northwards from the river to Seaton Carew, but today there are few signs of the derricks and associated buildings. The site of the former Bell Brothers works has also been cleared and most of the northern bank of the river below the Transporter Bridge has reverted to rough grassland.

Information for walkers

Several former industrial sites between Stockton and Middlesbrough have recently been cleared and landscaped with riverside walkways. The route is clearly marked and runs along level ground between the two towns.

From the lorry park on Stockton's Riverside Road, the path runs behind Castlegate Marine Club premises on to open ground and along the river bank past Portrack Marshes to the Newport Bridge. There is no path on the northern bank beyond this point and it is necessary to cross the bridge in order to join the path on the southern bank. The route follows the great curve in the river enclosing the former Ironmasters' District and skirts around Teessaurus Park, before linking up with the metalled road that runs behind several industrial premises to the viewing platform close to the Transporter Bridge. This point is said to mark the site of coal staithes constructed in 1830.

The impressive outlines of the Transporter Bridge have dominated the river landscape at Middlesbrough since its opening in October 1911.

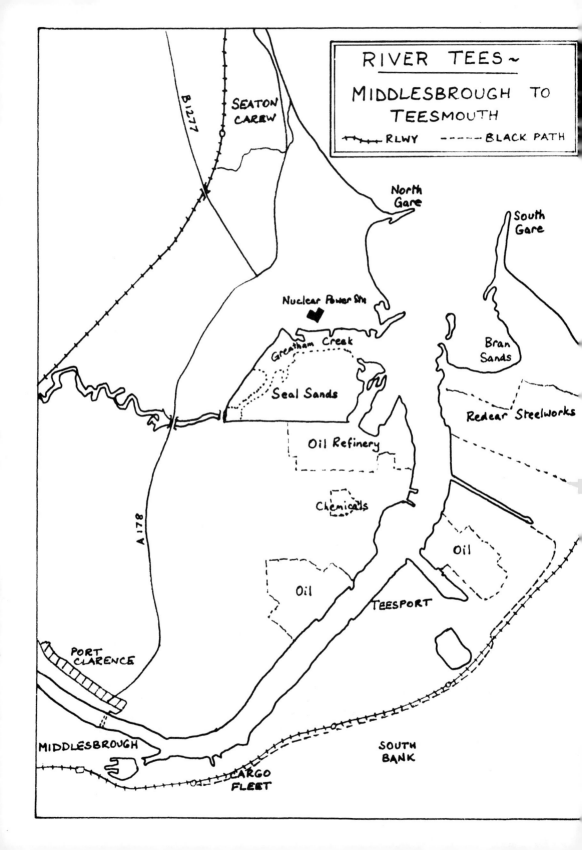

CHAPTER NINE

Middlesbrough Dock to Tees Dock

BELOW the Transporter Bridge the scene is constantly changing as businesses supporting the offshore oil and gas industries move on to land formerly occupied by shipyards and heavy industry. Close to the bridge on its southern side, much of the river frontage has been used in recent years for construction of modules for North Sea industries by Davy Offshore Modules and also Whessoe Ltd. The only reminder of Middlesbrough's early days is a section of the south end wall of the Cleveland Salt Works, which operated from 1887 to 1947. This imposing length of brickwork was restored during the early nineteen-eighties to highlight several oval-shaped windows and the central doorway.

In 1837 the owners of the Middlesbrough Estate and the Stockton and Darlington Railway Company drew up plans for a dock scheme on the southern bank. William Cubitt was engaged as engineer, land was purchased in 1839 and excavation work began during the following year. Water was first channelled into the dock on 19th March, 1842, and it opened for business on 12th May. The original water area of nine acres was extended in 1869, 1885 and 1895 to give a total of over twenty-five acres with ten berths. Access from the main river course was through an entrance channel, which was crossed by a swing bridge. This was manufactured at Sir William Armstrong's works on the Tyne. Ships of up to about 17,500 dwt were handled at the berths—depending on suitable tides —during the post war years. In summer 1980 the Tees and Hartlepool Port Authority closed Middlesbrough Dock (see chapter ten). Several of the Dock's newer cranes were transferred to Tees Dock and seventeen others, weighing between 54 and 110 tonnes, were cut up for scrap.

A sector of Middlesbrough Dock was reopened by THPA during the late nineteen-eighties as the Cleveland Wharves, but schemes are currently being considered (in early 1990) for the redevelopment of this whole area of land between the river and Middlesbrough town centre with housing and commercial premises, a major new hospital complex and buildings for Durham University.

The Dock Tower remains as a prominent landmark and a reminder of the Dock's busy times. The present brick tower, which replaced the original structure of 1842, has a clock face on three of its four sides and several improbable explanations for the failure to include the fourth face. Among the suggestions put forward were that the builders ran out of money, that employers did not want a face where their workers could see it less they were tempted to "clock watch", and that employees and employers refused to contribute to the fourth face. The river frontage below the entrance to Middlesbrough is highlighted by the outlines of Tees Towing Company's operations centre and their fleet of harbour tugs. The Tees Towing Co. Ltd was formed in 1920 by the amalgamation of the two largest towage companies on the River Tees, the Tees Tug Co. Ltd and the Robinson Tug Co. Ltd. The controlling interest soon passed into the hands of the Crosthwaite family. William Crosthwaite and his son, Cecil, kept the fleet in existence during difficult years in the nineteen-twenties and thirties, and since 1945 a number of important improvements and developments have been completed. In 1962 the company achieved an all-diesel fleet of vessels which had all been constructed to their own requirements. Recent additions to the fleet were built with the revolutionary rudder propellers which allowed greater manoeuvrability and fuel economy on the narrow, deep waters of the Tees.

Tees Towing Company's fleet of tugs berthed on the southern bank at the company's headquarters.

Cleveland Port

Cargo Fleet was originally known as Caldecoates and then as Calcoate Fleet. This tiny community flourished on the south bank of the Tees during the medieval period, when it became a busy port, along with Coatham and Dabholme further downstream. Until dredging operations got under way in the mid-nineteenth century, only small vessels could negotiate the shifting sands and shallow waters to reach Yarm and Stockton. Many large ships loaded and unloaded cargoes at Cleveland Port (as this settlement became known) for re-shipment. Exports largely consisted of dairy produce, such as butter and cheese, and imports were made up of commodities including coal, lime and timber. Nearby mudflats provided a plentiful supply of mussels to supplement the diet of local inhabitants.

Exploitation of iron ore deposits in the Cleveland Hills after 1850 and construction of the rail link between Middlesbrough and Redcar which opened on 4th June, 1846, brought rapid industrialization along this final stretch of the southern bank. Construction of ironworks was followed by completion of housing for the workforce and their families. In 1872 Arthur Warner established new works at Cargo Fleet to exploit the manufacturing of a special brand of cast iron in the form of "pigs". The first reference to Cleveland Port appears in 1733 and this small settlement was later known as Caldecoates. The recent name, Cargo Fleet, appears to have been a product of late nineteenth-century industrial development. Sadler and Company had moved on to a one and a half acre site at Cargo Fleet in 1868. They specialized in the distillation of tar and were the first firm to extract and market benzene. Other products that they supplied included acids, ammonia, potash and superphosphates. By 1930 the company premises covered some sixteen acres and during the post war years the company played an important part in the development of petrochemicals on Teesside. This period also saw the development of an industrial estate in Cargo Fleet Lane, and the Cleveland Product Company moved on to a site close to the river where they produced a variety of goods including gelatine, di-calcium phosphate and dripping. A thriving community spirit characterized the rows of terraced properties at Cargo Fleet, but during the late nineteen-seventies this housing was cleared. The only remaining buildings from Cleveland Port had already been lost in 1974 when properties on Prospect Place and Customs Row were demolished.

A community also grew up at South Bank during the second half of the nineteenth century after Bernhard Samuelson leased a ten-acre field for building plots in 1855. A range of amenities was provided for the workforce, many of whom came from Ireland; strong Roman Catholic traditions continue to the present day. Employment was available in local ironworks, and in the early nineteen-hundreds a major development took shape when Smith's Dock Co. Ltd of North and South Shields erected a large shipbuilding yard. Operations began in 1909–10 and building and repair work continued until in the early nineteen-eighties the Trade and Industry Secretary, Paul Channon, announced that the yard was to close. The 15,000-tonne *North Islands* was the last vessel to be launched at Smith's Dock on 15th October, 1986, and a workforce numbering 1,295 was left to search for alternative employment during the following spring when British Shipbuilders closed the gates for the last time. Attempts to reopen the yard came to nothing and workshops and facilities were acquired by THPA, who currently operate it as Tees Offshore. Parts of the nearby township have been redeveloped in recent years with an improved road network and completion of a major superstore. Many industrial eyesores have been removed under reclamation and landscaping schemes and residents look with pride on local folk who have achieved fame in different walks of life. Numbered among these are international footballers Jackie Carr and Wilf Mannion, entertainers such as Jimmy James and Paul Daniels, opera singer Florence Easton and record-breaking parachutist Jackie Smith.

Tees Dock

Tees Dock is an open tidal dock on the southern bank some three and a half miles from the river mouth. Constructed in 1963, it has five general cargo berths along two quays with four single-storey transit sheds providing about 30,000 square metres of storage space. The Steel Export Terminal became operational in November, 1976. Owned by British Steel and operated by THPA, it can handle up to a million tonnes of steel per year and has two berths with a quay frontage of three hundred metres. A ro ro berth at the inland end of the dock was opened in 1973 and is able to handle up to four lanes of traffic simultaneously. It deals mainly with containers and trailers, but can also be used by car ships. The Bulk Cargo Terminal was built by THPA and leased to Teesbulk Handling Ltd. It handles a range of bulk materials, including potash, coal and grain.

Much of the recent development on both banks of the Tees has taken place on reclaimed land. Former mudflats have been drained and filled in to provide extra dock and storage facilities. In early February, 1990, work began on an £8 million extension of the Tees container terminal. This joint venture between THPA and container shipping operator, Bell Lines Ltd, will more than double the size of the existing quay at the terminal to cater for increased services to Rotterdam and Rouen. Adjacent land is covered by the extensive Nissan terminal, which is made up of a fifteen-acre export site and a fifty-eight-acre import site that can hold up to 10,000 cars. The terminal, which currently handles over 100,000 cars per year, worth over £750 million, is set to expand as Nissan's Sunderland factory increases its European operations after 1992, with over 400,000 cars per year passing through the terminal.

Tidal mudflats on the north bank of the river have been systematically reclaimed over the last twenty years to provide large tracts of land for industrial use. Bitmac Ltd occupy land downstream from the Transporter Bridge, and adjacent riverside land is covered by the storage tanks of ICI North Tees and PIP Refinery. BASF is a subsidiary of one of the world's largest chemical companies. Over five hundred people are employed at its Seal Sands site in the manufacture of chemical intermediates, and in February, 1990, the firm announced plans for a £6 million investment programme to provide a new building for technical units and process development.

The Seal Sands site on the Tees estuary's northern side also provides an ideal base for Phillips Petroleum Company's operations in the North Sea. Oil and gas liquids from the Ekofisk field are pumped through a 220-mile pipeline to the terminal at Seal Sands where they are separated. Crude oil is loaded on to tankers at adjacent deep-water berths for shipment to refineries in Western

Indian Faith, moored at No 6 berth, Tees Dock.

Europe and elsewhere. Some crude oil is also piped to the nearby Phillips Imperial Petroleum Refinery at North Tees—see reference to PIP Refinery in previous paragraph. Natural liquid gases are further separated into methane, ethane, propane and butane.

Information for walkers

There is no public access to the former Middlesbrough Dock, but a former sailors' trod that runs from Cargo Fleet Station along the south side of the Middlesbrough to Redcar Railway offers a chance to view industry and wildlife along this final stretch of the river.

This pathway probably became known as the Black Path after 1855 as parts of it were gradually covered by cinders and grime from nearby blast furnaces. It is possible to follow the path for about five miles before joining the A1085 trunk road from Middlesbrough to Redcar where a bus service links up with the starting point near Cargo Fleet Station.

A leaflet describing the route is available from Cleveland County Department of Economic Development and Planning, Gurney House, Middlesbrough TS1 1QT.

Stena Apache, cable-laying vessel, berthed in the Tees during February 1990.

CHAPTER TEN

The Tees Estuary

CARGO handling and management of vessels on the Tees is controlled by the Tees and Hartlepool Port Authority. Set up as an independent statutory body in 1966, the Port Authority's jurisdiction extends from the highest tidal point, some twenty-five miles inland, to the Fairway Buoy, which is stationed about three miles offshore in Tees Bay. About 30 million tonnes of cargo are handled annually on the Tees by a total workforce of 1,100, including 450 registered dockworkers. Since the early nineteen-sixties the total tonnage volume through the port has increased from less than ten million to this figure of around thirty million tonnes. Sophisticated radar equipment at the Traffic Management Centre monitors all movements on the river and the Port Authority owns a number of specialist vessels to ensure that safety and smooth-running is maintained. The *Wilton*, a £2 million buoy tender vessel was launched in September, 1983, and services the fifty buoys in the river and its approaches. Modern suction dredgers, *Heortnesse* and *Cleveland County* and a grab dredger, the *Seal Sands*, remove up to three million cubic metres per year from the river channel while hydrographic survey work is carried out by two launches, *Tees Soundsman* and *Tees Surveyor*. In summer 1986 the Port Authority commissioned a new harbour patrol launch. Costing £270,000, it has a top speed of 18 knots and a range of 300 nautical miles.

The jutting steelwork of Redcar Ore Terminal dominates the southern bank below Tees Dock. Opened in 1973 at a cost of £23 million, it is a joint venture between British Steel and the THPA. Three giant unloaders can work on ships of up to 150,000 dead weight tonnage (dwt) with a handling capacity of around 10 million tonnes of coal and coke annually. Raw materials are stacked and blended before being fed into production plants by conveyor systems and then charged to the nearby Redcar furnace, the largest in Europe.

On the northern bank Greatham Creek feeds the wide estuary. The most prominent landmark on this low-lying expanse of former mudflats is Hartlepool Power Station. Built by the Nuclear Power Company (Whetstone) Ltd and operated by the Central Electricity Generating Board, it first supplied electricity to the grid in 1972, some four years after construction work began. Hartlepool Energy Information Centre is sited near the power station. A computer-controlled audio-visual show explains the story of local energy and electricity generation.

Until dredging operations created a main channel for sea-going vessels, the mouth of the river consisted of extensive mudflats and shifting sands. By 1900 more than half of Teesmouth's 2,400 hectares of inter-tidal mudflats had been reclaimed by industrial use and during the nineteen-sixties and nineteen-

Hartlepool power station dominates the low-lying ground on the northern bank close to the river mouth.

seventies much of the remaining land was also developed. A fierce debate raged between industrialists and conservationists as the habitats of plants, animals, birds and insects were again threatened in the early nineteen-eighties, but a workable compromise was reached. Little more than 160 hectares of mudflats remain at Teesmouth, but there is a whole range of life to be found here at each state of the tide. A green algae, *Enteromorpha*, grows on the open mud, and bladderwrack, a brown seaweed, clings to stonework around the tidal flats. Ragworm and lugworm live in the soft surface mud, along with molluscs such as cockles and tellins, while shore crabs scavenge along the high-water mark. Seal Sands derives its name from the common seals which used to breed there in large numbers. In recent years grey seals have outnumbered common seals on the mudflats and sandbanks of the estuary and are often to be seen basking on the shoreline or breaking the water's surface. Much of the outcry over loss of mudflats at Teesmouth has centred around the importance of this area as the only feeding area for transient and migratory birds on England's east coast between the Humber Estuary and Fenham Flats. Seal Sands are now listed as a Grade One Site of Special Scientific Interest and forty-six species of wading birds have been recorded. Many of these species are present at Teesmouth in December each year when up to 15,000 birds gather on the feeding ground, but it was on 31st August, 1982, that a tiny wader—a juvenile long-toed stint—drew

BASF Jetty—dealing with chemical products.

birdwatchers from all over the country. Measuring about thirteen centimetres in length, it normally breeds in Siberia before migrating to parts of Australasia for the winter months. Its appearance at Seal Sands represented the first sighting of a long-toed stint in the British Isles. More than thirty-two species of wildfowl have been recorded at Teesmouth and restrictions on shooting, together with other factors, have resulted in greater numbers than last century. On the southern bank close to the ore terminal a "pink" goat provided a talking point for some time during the nineteen-eighties—its white fur or skin pigment turned "pink" by dust from the nearby terminal. During the nineteen-seventies a flamingo graced the lakes and mudflats close to factories on the northern bank. For some eight years it spent most of the year among these industrial sites, leaving only for a short summer vacation.

North and South Gare

The entrance to the Tees Estuary is marked by breakwaters on either side of the mouth—North and South Gare. Following serious shipping losses along this stretch of coastline, in February, 1861, plans were put forward for a port of refuge just south of Teesmouth at Redcar. This scheme for "Port William" was not followed through, but loans were arranged for wo' on breakwaters at either side of the estuary. South Gare is some two and a half miles in length and construction work lasted from 1863 to 1888 at a total cost of £219,393. Some seven million tons of slag from nearby blast furnaces was moved by rail to form the basis of the concrete-covered structure. Features on South Gare include Paddy's Hole—a small man-made harbour—lifeboat station, pilots' station and "tacky shades", which measure dust in the atmosphere. The seaward end is dominated by the coastguard station and radio mast along with a foghorn and lighthouse. An explanatory leaflet about South Gare is available from the Cleveland County Planning Department in Middlesbrough.

North Gare is half a mile long and was constructed between 1882 and 1891 at a cost of £65,531. At low tide the wooden remains of sunken vessels are exposed alongside both breakwaters as a reminder of the hazards that faced ships entering the Tees in earlier years. It is not compulsory to employ the services of a pilot on the Tees, but one of the three pilot cutters (*High Force, White Force* and *Alderman B. O. Davies*) can often be seen ferrying officers to and from sea-going vessels. THPA's powers extend as far as the Fairway Buoy some three miles out into Tees Bay, where ships turn into the main channel. The present buoy was towed into position in 1982 and was said to be the largest of its type in the world. It cost £45,000 and stands nine metres above sea level.

Plans for a tunnel under the Tees were finally abandoned in 1983, but several controversial issues are being debated during 1990. Legislation is currently under consideration in Parliament to allow for the privatization of the Tees and Hartlepool Port Authority, plans for toxic waste incinerators on sites at Portrack and Seal Sands have also aroused considerable local opposition and members of the "Greenpeace" movement continue to highlight serious pollution problems linked to major industrial sites along the Tees.

Positive moves are being made to reduce levels of pollution in the lower reaches of the Tees and there are encouraging signs that migratory fish are returning to the river. The recent establishment of a Tees Valley Warden Service has led to greater public interest in, and awareness of, the varied natural history associated with the river; on-going plans to create a long-distance walkway may soon allow members of the public to appreciate at first hand the range of natural and historical features along the course of this fascinating north country river.

Information for walkers

There is no access to the river banks along this final stretch of the Tees. The public are allowed to visit both North Gare and South Gare, but are asked to keep to the car parks and viewing areas. (Both Gares and the approach roads are owned by British Steel and the Tees and Hartlepool Port Authority.)

*   *   *

The meeting of the waters. Countless artists and writers have captured this scene where the Greta joins the Tees close to Rokeby.

Bibliography

General

Bailey, R. N. *Viking Age Sculpture*. Collins Archaeology, 1980.
Barbey, M. F. *Civil Engineering Heritage*. Thomas Telford Ltd, 1981.
Bellamy, D. *The Tees—The Living River*. David Bellamy Associates, 1988.
Brown, M. M. and Still, L. *Cleveland History from the Air*. Cleveland County Libraries, 1980.
Clapham, A. R. (ed.) *Upper Teesdale: The Area and its Natural History, 1978*.
The River Tees: Two centuries of Change (Album of plans with descriptive notes), 1990.
Coggins, D. *Teesdale in Old Photographs*, Alan Sutton, 1989.
Durham County Council, *The Durham Book*, Durham County Council, 1980.
Fletcher, J. S. *The Enchanted North*, Eveleigh Nash, 1908.
Fraser, C. and Emsley, K. *Northumbria*, Phillimore Ltd, 1989.
Heavisides, M. *Rambles by the River Tees*, M. T. D. Rigg Publications, 1989.
Hellier, D. S. *The History of the Tees Pilots*, Tees Pilot Authority, 1982.
Johnson, G. A. L. *The Geology of Moor House*, HMSO, 1963.
Le Guillou, M. *A History of the River Tees*. Cleveland County Libraries, 1978.
Mee, A. *The King's England: Durham*. Hodder and Stoughton, 1953.
Mee, A. *The King's England: Yorkshire North Riding*, Hodder and Stoughton, 1950.
Mitchell, W. R. *Pennine Birds*. Dalesman Books, 1978.
Mitchell, W. R. *Pennine Lead Miner*. Dalesman Books, 1979.
Parker, M. *Stories, Sketches and Places to Visit in Teesdale*. Discovery Guides Ltd, 1980.
Pevsner, N. *The Buildings of England: Durham*. Penguin, 1983.
Pevsner, N. *The Buildings of England: Yorkshire North Riding*. Penguin, 1978.
Proud, J. H. *Seahorses of the Tees*. Tees Towing Company Ltd, 1985.
Ramsden, D. M. *Teesdale*. Museum Press Ltd, 1947.
Watson, R. *Poems and Songs of Teesdale*. W. Dresser and Sons, 1930.
Wedgwood, I. *Northumberland and Durham*. Faber and Faber, 1932.
Wood, B. *North Country Profile*. Country Life Ltd, 1961.

Places

Barnard Castle
  Barnard Castle—A Guide to the Town and Neighbourhood. Barnard Castle Publicity Society
    and Chamber of Trade, 1951.
Middlesbrough
  Briggs, A. *Victorian Cities*. Penguin Books, 1980.
  Lillie, W. *Middlesbrough*. Middlesbrough Corporation, 1968.
  Moorsom, B. *The Book of Middlesbrough*. Barracuda Books Ltd, 1986.
  Dawson, A. G. *Middlesbrough Transporter Bridge—A History*. 1986.
Middleton-in-Teesdale
  Heavisides, M. *Guide to the Walks around Middleton-in-Teesdale*. Local Council Publication,
    1920.
  A New Guide to Middleton-in-Teesdale & District. Middleton in Teesdale and District
    Chamber of Trade, 1985.
Moor House
  Moor House National Nature Reserve, A Guide. Nature Conservancy Council, 1975.

Piercebridge
    Selkirk, R. *The Piercebridge Formula*. Patrick Stephens Ltd, 1975.
Stockton   Sowler, T. *A History of the Town and Borough of Stockton-on-Tees*. Teesside Museums Art Galleries Dept, 1972.
    Woodhouse, R. *Stockton: A Pictorial History*. Phillimore Ltd, 1989.
Teesmouth
    The Birds of Teesmouth. Teesmouth Bird Club. (Annual publication.)
Teesdale
    Upper Teesdale National Widdybank Fell Nature Trail. Nature Conservancy Council Nature Reserve, 1980.
Worsall
    Barton, P. *Low Worsall, The Shipping and Trade of an Eighteenth Century Port on the River Tees, Mariner's Mirror*, vol. 55, no 1.
Wycliffe
    History of Wycliffe. Available from Wycliffe church.

People

Matheson, B. D. *The Tender Years—Lewis Carroll around the North*. Nordale Publications, 1984.
Woodhouse, R. *Cleveland's Hall of Fame and Infamy*. E. W. Harrison and Son Ltd, 1986.

Industry

The Mines and Minerals of Teesdale and Weardale. Cleveland County Museum Service, 1984.
Harrison, J. K. and Almond, J. *Industrial Archaeology in Cleveland*. Cleveland County Libraries, 1978.
North, G. *Teesside's Economic Heritage*. Cleveland County Council, 1975.
Tomlin, D. M. *Past Industry along the Tees*. A. A. Sotheran Ltd, 1980.

Index